4-28-75

CHILDREN AND DYING

An Exploration and Selective Bibliographies

by

SARAH SHEETS COOK, R.N.

with additional essays by

KARL D. BUDMEN, DOMEENA RENSHAW, STUART MIL-
STEIN, EDGAR JACKSON, EDWARD H. FUTTERMAN and
IRWIN HOFFMAN, DILLER B. GROFF, DALIA KEYSER,
ELIZABETH F. YOUNG, MARY F. ROBINSON, PHYLLIS R.
SILVERMAN, and EARL GROLLMAN

Compiled and Edited by Roberta Halporn

(Revised and Expanded Edition)

HEALTH SCIENCES PUBLISHING CORPORATION
NEW YORK, NEW YORK

1974

Library of Congress Cataloging in Publication Data

Sheets, Sarah L.

Children and dying.

1. Children and death. 2. Sick children—Psychology. 3. Children and death—Bibliography. I. Title. [DNLM: 1. Child psychology. 2. Child psychology—Bibliography. 3. Death. 4. Death—Bibliography. 5. Terminal care—In infancy and childhood. 6. Pediatric nursing. 7. Pediatric nursing—Bibliography. ZWS 105

RJ47.5.C66   1974   155.9'37   74-26698
ISBN 0-88238-539-9

Printed in the United States of America
MEILEN PRESS INC., NEW YORK, N.Y.

TABLE OF CONTENTS

HOW CHILDREN FEEL AND REACT TO DEATH

Childrens' Perceptions of Death

By Sarah Sheets Cook, R.N., B.S.N., M.Ed.*

> This paper was presented at the Symposium and Work-shop on "Psychosocial Aspects of Anticipatory Grief," sponsored by the
>
> Department of Psychiatry of the
> Faculty of Medicine, Columbia University
>
> and
>
> The Foundation of Thanatology
> April 14th, 1972
> New York, N.Y.

A little girl of four years was devoted to her kitty cat. One day the cat died. The family was concerned about the child's reaction, but she accepted explanations and condolences with equanimity until it came to the burial of the cat in the backyard. She then insisted that the kitty be buried in the flower garden. When asked why, she said, "Because then Kitty will come up every Spring with the flowers, and I can play with her again."—Dr. Elizabeth K. Ross[1]

One of the many problems in dealing with children and death or with the dying child is the tendency of adults to equate their perceptions of death with the child's perceptions. In investigating childrens' reactions to and perceptions of death, it becomes clearly evident that members of the helping professions must recognize and understand the distinction in order to deal with the more complex situation of the family and the dying child. It will be the intent of this paper to describe children's perceptions of death in

* Assistant Professor of Nursing, Department of Nursing, Faculty of Medicine, Columbia University, New York, New York.

1

general, and their perceptions of their own death in particular. Further, implications will be drawn for constructive nursing intervention. Etiology of terminal conditions, grief and grieving, parental reactions per se, and physical care of the dying child will not be discussed except as they relate to the child's perceptions.

Several interesting observations arise in effecting such a project. Almost all of the articles and books considered begin with the notion that death and children and the dying child are difficult subjects and important, but not that much has been written about it. However, when one begins to research a bibliography, the number of articles seems endless. It is as if each author must go through a long, researching process of his own in order to arrive at some opinion about the subject. Closer perusal of the material does indicate that there is a paucity of new material on the subject, and that many "new" articles (as this one) are a recombination and republication with editing of past work. (Maria Nagy's work appears originally in the *Journal of Genetic Psychology*, later in Herman Feifel's book, and is included in or alluded to in several anthologies on the subject of childrens' perceptions of death.) The earliest evidences of work in this area do not appear until the 1930's and early 1940's,[2,3,4] and then there is an absence of material until the late 1950's and early 1960's, when an explosion of material occurs. It is also of note, that with the exception of Jeanne Quint, the majority of work is done by physicians, psychologists, and psychiatrists. Even in articles about physical care of terminal children (the nature of the bulk of nursing articles), there is little reference to the subject of children's perceptions.

In the '60's, when Yudkin, Vernick and Karon, Solnit and Green, Natterson and Knudson, etc., mention intervention, they speak of physician's intervention, not necessarily nurse's. All this would seem to indicate a stage of mass professional denial, which is just beginning to be broken through (in the '60's, we begin to see some articles in nursing journals about teaching concepts of dying to students, and Jeanne Quint's book, *The Nurse and the Dying Patient* only appeared in 1967). One might say that the medical profession as a whole is in a state of identity crisis with respect to care of the dying—no one is really quite sure what his role is, especially nurses. At a recent conference on The Dying Patient, (Columbia University, College of Physicians and Surgeons, 4/69), many speakers felt the problem stemmed from the very nature of medical care in this country—we are oriented toward cure, rather than care, comfort or prevention. Death, and especially the death of a child, in such an atmosphere, becomes an enemy. A personal vendetta with death develops on the part of the physician and nurse in that when death 'wins,' doubt, guilt and questions are cast on the ability of the professional person—a kind of "Somehow I've failed to perform my job successfully" attitude. As Robert Fulton succinctly puts it:

> In our modern, secular society, death is coming to be seen as the result of personal negligence or of an unforeseen accident . . . Death, like a noxious disease, has become a taboo subject in American society and as such it is the object of much avoidance, denial and disgust.[5]

And further, by Simon Yudkin:

> The death of a child from an illness . . . is an affront to our pride. Our job is to prevent or cure disease, not to accommodate with death; the more successful we are, the more our comparatively few failures produce in us a deep emotional reaction.[6]

Perhaps the more basic issue is the consistent human inability, markedly present in professional people, to accept human fallibility.

That childrens' perceptions of death are related to their developmental level is hardly a surprising fact, although in the stress of dealing with a dying child, it is frequently forgotten or denied. Robert Kastenbaum[7] makes some interesting observations about death 'perceptions' in infants and toddlers. Such an age group obviously has no concrete conception of death, but there is the possibility that certain experiences and behaviors may help the child to begin to relate to a state of nonbeing. In reporting the work of Adah Maurer, he points out that an infant's perceptions of differences between sleeping and waking begin the development of appreciation of being and nonbeing. The young infant's response to having a diaper placed over his face is discussed, and the meaning of the old game "peek-a-boo" is re-questioned. Maurer points out that "peek-a-boo" comes from the Old English, meaning "alive or dead." Such a game and others which provide experiences in "disappearance and return" are seen as experiments with nonbeing or death, and a way of development of concepts of separation and autonomy. Kastenbaum says:

Perhaps the toddler is experimenting with the experiences of separation, loss and nonbeing more than we realize. Perhaps these experiences provide the foundations for his later conceptions. Perhaps as Maurer and some others have suggested, these very early flirtations with death play an important role in the child's general mental, emotional and social development (p. 96).

Maria Nagy did one of the first and perhaps most comprehensive studies of childrens' perceptions of death.[8] Her work has been criticized by Morrisey[9] and others as being representative of only one socioeconomic and cultural group, but her study or any like it has never been replicated in any other group, except by Rochlin.[10] The advantage of these two studies over those of the nature of Solnit and Green,[11] Binger,[12] and Natterson and Knudson[13] seems to be that the children studied were not threatened by their own impending death, thereby giving a more natural developmental viewpoint. Nagy reports:

> The child of less than five years does not recognize death as an irreversible fact. In death it sees life. Between the ages of five and nine, death is most often personified and thought of as a contingency. And in general, only after the age of nine, is it recognized that death is a process happening to us according to certain laws.[14]

In Nagy's sample of children under five, the children attributed life and consciousness to the dead. One group saw death as a departure or sleep, a complete denial of death; while another group recognized death as an entity but could not separate it from life. For the death departure group dying meant going away, but no change in the status of the departing one—only in those left who will see him no longer.

Nagy, as most others, found that the most painful aspect at this age was separation. Even if a child is familiar with cemeteries, funerals, burials, etc. (occasions foreign to most children this age in this country), they still felt that the deceased continued to live, but in the confines of the coffin, where he breathes, eats and knows what is going on in the world outside.[15] In the group of children of five to six who did not deny death, there are still perceptual problems in terms of seeing death as a gradual or temporary phenomenon. In this state, life and death are interchangeable, simultaneous. Nagy feels that this is the next or at least a higher level of development and that there is at least a beginning distinction of the two processes.

In discussing the death/departure group, Nagy poses the question as to why, at this young age, opposition to death is so strong that the child denies it. The question becomes interesting in terms of Gregory Rochlin's work with three to five year olds. Rochlin carries Nagy's work to greater depths. He corroborates her findings (with American children) that this age group finds death reversible; that when someone dies, they continue to grow, they get hungry and eat. Excremental functions, as well as locomotion, continue.[16]

He distinguishes between recognition of death as absence of life and philosophic acceptance of this fact. He feels young children are cognizant of the former but not of the latter.[17] The psychological defenses at this age cause "an alteration in subjective experiences in order to overcome helplessness and sense of loss through fantasies of omnipotence and invulnerability."[18] This leads to denial and refusal to accept the finality of death.

Rochlin revives Freud's ideas about narcissism as an explanation of this denial. He recounts the developmental characteristic of this age group: belief in omnipotence of wishes and power of magic, imperishable egocentricity, sense of helplessness coupled with dependence on others in authority, a deep and pervasive concern with causality.[19] Then:

> I have tried to show that the painful facts that people die, that limitations of one's powers exist . . . are all evident to the very young child. It appears that these threats to life and this recognition of reality are joined by the development of narcissism. The more closely death is encountered or limits to one's person confronted, either early in life or as its end approaches, the more narcissism is relied upon.[20]

Recognition of this process seems especially important not only in dealing with the death of children but also with adults. Again Rochlin:

> In crisis, they [more intellectually derived values] are quickly deposed to give way to the older, more firmly established values of childhood.[21]

This would seem to have implication for nursing care to be discussed later.

Nagy and Kastenbaum both comment on the second developmental stage of thanatologic attitudes in children from about five to nine years. Kastenbaum says . . . "there is the impression that in mid-childhood the youth can neither deny or accept death as an authentic aspect of his own life. Some kind of compromise is necessary."[22]

Death for this age becomes a personification, a distinct personality. Children either create their own image or accept the more traditional one of the 'skeleton man.' He is usually invisible, meaning either without form, or going about at night so he cannot be seen. Even at this stage, although there is a higher level of integration than before, death is still remote—it exists, but outside one's self and through careful living, it can be kept at a distance.[23]

It is not until the age of nine or ten years that the adult concept of death appears. The child realizes that death, including his own, is an inevitable process, with the perceptible result that the bodily life ends. Kastenbaum again points out concomitant developmental traits:[24] children of this age are better able to recognize the difference between animate and inanimate on a logical thought basis (Piaget), egocentricity is less, and concepts of time, space, quantity and causality are set. By this age children have had sufficient experience in learning what it means to be alive and can appreciate and understand not being alive. "Death can be understood in relation to 'natural law' in general, it is no longer a phantom or will o' the wisp."[25]

There is not a great deal of information about adolescent perceptions of death. Most authors have been content to bring the child to the age of nine or ten, at which time 'adult' perceptions take over. But adolescents are not adults. Robert Kastenbaum[26] has done observant work in the area. He considers the nature of the adolescent—the search for identity, the multitude of "new selves" with which to be experimented, the rapid transformations to be experienced in every sphere—physical, social, emotional, cognitive. The adolescent is aware of himself emotionally as an individual and has the intellectual tools—power to view, preview and review life, to think deeply about death but finds it a natural enemy at a time when he is so concerned about life and living. The adolescent is in a pivotal position; his maturing outlook on life and death is

strongly influenced by the existing cultural matrix, and the re-
sultant configuration of personal beliefs strongly influences future
experiences.[27]

Kastenbaum also brings up an interesting point about adolescents
and time perceptions:[28]

1. The adolescent lives in an intense present, "now" is so real
    to him that both past and future are pallid in comparison.
    Everything that is valuable and important in life lies in
    the immediate life situation or the very near future.

2. Extremely little explicit structure is given to the remote
    future; attitudes toward the distal regions of subjective
    life . . . are distinctly negative; 15, 16, 17 year olds see
    the remote future as risky and devoid of significant positive
    values.

3. More explicit structure is given to the past than the remote
    future, but the past is also risky and unpleasant, a vague
    confusing place where the adolescent was not at all sure of
    personal identity.

Thus, although the adolescent is capable of considering death
in adult terms and may think about it, death tends to be considered a remote possibility or if obviously present, disliked because
it comes at a time when living is so intense and so important.
Jersild also brings up the situation of adolescent fantasy about death
—that they will always be rescued at the last minute and go on
living.[29] Again, these ideas seem to have implications for nursing
intervention. As Yudkin points out, despite the time perception
phenomenon of the adolescent, this age is more likely to adjust to
fatality with the same defenses of an adult.[30]

An interesting philosophic point emerges when one considers
whether or not a child, at any age and at any level of perception
of death, is really able to perceive or conceive his own death.
Does it necessarily follow that because a child "perceives" death
of others—grandparents, pets, etc., he also is capable of perceiv-
ing his own death? Most authors come to the conclusion in a
round-about fashion; that the child does or can perceive his own
death, but in terms of the developmental level he is at and through
the catalyst of some crisis event, such as catastrophic illness.

Morrisey's study of age and death anxiety[31] showed that there
was a strong relationship between increasing age and expressed

death anxiety in relation to illness. He found that children up to the age of nine expressed death anxiety in terms of separation and/or mutilation/castration fears and children older than nine expressed direct fear of death. He feels that young children often experience emotions without verbalizing or conceptualizing the feelings involved and are prone to symbolization and physiologic expression of the anxiety. Older boys tend to act out, and older girls are prone to depression.[32] Also, most of the "classic" authors previously mentioned—Solnit and Green, Binger, Natterson and Knudson, have done their work primarily with leukemic children, certainly a catastrophic illness, which tends to support the original hypotheses.

Another aspect of this problem is the professional person's ability to interpret the child's perceptions. Solnit and Green say:

> It has become apparent that a more systematic investigation of the child's psychological reactions to his own dying will have to take into account the adult's tendency not to perceive the dying child's behavioral and verbal communications about his own fears because of the anxieties evoked in the adult by the dying child.[33]

Solnit continues:

> The child who is dying of a fatal illness arouses in himself and his family, as well as in the physician and others who care for him, the most fearful and resentful awareness of uncertainty and loss.[34]

Binger mentions the conflicts, anxieties and guilt experienced by the professional in dealing with dying children, which leads to avoidance, facades of busyness, unapproachability, impatience or formality.[35] George Engel brings up a particular problem for female nurses in relation to the dying child:

> Because it is so inherent in her psychology as a woman, the nurse is likely to be more emotionally involved in the loss of a child than of an adult patient, and she may be upset when the mother's reaction differs from her own or from her expectation of what it should be.[36]

In terms of implications for nursing intervention, it becomes immediately evident that the nurse must assess and understand the individual child's perception of death, at whatever developmental level. Further he or she must be aware of how his or her own feelings and perceptions can influence his judgments. For example, the nurse must realize that the dying child who becomes extremely narcissistic and ego-centered is not necessarily spoiled, and that while certain limits for behavior are security-provoking, part of the behavior is the child's way of coping. The nurse must realize that children other than the child with a fatal illness may have anxieties about death.

Yudkin points out that children with acute illnesses, even if their main concern is fear of pain, separation or mutilation, may have death anxieties. He provides a definite list of symptoms for professionals to be aware of:[37] depression, lack of interest, unprovoked anger and resentment toward physician and staff, resentment toward parents if the child is old enough not to be affected by mere separation, denial of symptoms obviously present.

For the older child who is dying, especially the adolescent, the nurse must recognize that behavior patterns will be somewhat similar to those of adults. Dr. Elizabeth K. Ross has a rather unique way of classifying stages of 'acceptance' of death, which would seem essential for all nurses to know:[38]

1. "not me"—denial and shock

2. "why me"—anger, irritability, nastiness

3. "perhaps me, but . . ."—bargaining, "If I do this, I'll get better," etc.

4. "it is me"—depression, but beginning acceptance

5. "OK"—true acceptance, conscious decathexis and separation from loved ones

Failure to recognize these stages or active or covert blocking of expressing the various stages or talking about them, in adults or children, is cruel and certainly not helpful in fostering the most positive resolution possible. It is also important for the nurse to recognize that these stages do not always occur in the same sequence for every patient.

In dealing with the child who is dying, the question of "to tell or not to tell" always arises. Most authors believe it is not a question of to tell or not to tell, but *when* to tell. When a diagnosis of terminal illness has been made, ALL patients know, whether told or not, that something is seriously wrong. Yudkin points out that no matter how parents try to hide the fact or protect their children from the diagnosis, they cannot cover the changes in their own behavior. Younger children become confused at parental reaction and may feel that they did something horrible to upset their parents. If the parents overindulge the child, in addition to dealing with his own perceptions of what is wrong with him, he becomes even more frightened and more demanding in behavior.[39]

Older children may feel that if their parents cannot talk about what is happening, the child must protect the parent, even though he is fully aware of what is happening. Binger states that the loneliest dying children of all were those who were aware of their diagnosis but also recognized that their parents did not want them to know and thus were unable to communicate.[40] Vernick and Karon found that in every instance, when parents were told the diagnosis, the child 'knew' because of parental reaction.[41] In instances where children (all children older than 9 years and some younger) were told of their diagnosis, commensurate with their ages and background, every child accepted the explanation without untoward reaction, and many with relief. Families reported that they had a more meaningful relationship than ever before with their children because of openness of communication.[42] The implication for professional intervention seems strong: that the staff must help parents to come to terms with their feelings and also to realize those of their children. As previously mentioned, most of the articles quoted are written for physicians, but it would seem that there is an even stronger mandate toward this type of "family intervention" for nurses, since they are the ones who (could) spend most time with the child and family. Further implications are drawn for administrator/supervisors and faculty in terms of how free nurses are to implement such an approach and how is the generic student prepared to carry out such a role.

"How to tell" becomes a point for careful consideration. That the nature of the explanation is related to the individual situation and the developmental level of the child has already been mentioned. Solnit and Green point out that children are mostly concerned with three questions in relation to dying: "Am I safe?," "Will there be a trusted person to keep me from feeling helpless, alone, and to overcome pain?," and "Will you make me feel all right?"[43] Yudkin points out that young children are most concerned about discomfort and terror of symptomatology; that three to seven year olds are prone to fantasizing and become fearful of the fantasies; and that older children are fearful of suffering.[44]

Specific support by word or action can be given by the nurse in answer to these questions, whether voiced or implied by the child. To provide the support the nurse must be a careful and "unbiased" (in terms of her own feelings) observer and an attentive listener, especially in dealing with fantasies. It becomes a great human temptation to look for comic relief in tense situations, and childrens' fantasies frequently provide this relief for staff. It would seem especially important to be cognizant of the meaning and function of fantasy in this situation, as a key to the understanding and trust of the child. Parents frequently do not know how or are emotionally unable to think of a way to answer questions or talk to their children in this situation. The nurse often can foster communication between parent and child by providing a role model for the mother, but many nurses feel they should not intrude.

Solnit speaks about the physician being involved in this process, but it would seem to apply to the nurse also:

> The physician will gain an impression of how to be most helpful to a particular child by gauging the tolerances and preferred ways of coping with life expressed by the patient and his family, as well as by understanding the range of customs and social values transmitted to them by their culture and religious beliefs.[45]

Another measure for supportively reducing feelings of helplessness is mentioned by Vernick and Karon:[46] gaining "consent" for procedures from the child himself by sharing medical information with him, relative to his age. Older schoolage children and adolescents especially are interested and can understand fairly complex descriptions of what is happening to them. They recount the story of H., a 14 year old, who said in relation to a liver biopsy: "They called my mother to get permission. I know it's necessary, but I'm mad my doctor didn't talk to me about it—it's *my* liver. What am I, some sort of rat or something?" Even though medical and nursing procedures are "supposed" to be explained, this is frequently forgotten. It would seem nurses miss an opportunity for further communication by such omissions.

Vernick and Karon point out that professionals must encourage and help parents discuss the diagnosis with their dying child, not only to preserve an open, trusting relationship between parent and child, but also in terms of the effect on siblings, and the total family relationship.[47] Siblings may perceive as quickly or quicker than the ill child that something is wrong. They may resent the special treatment the child receives with subsequent development of misunderstandings and jealousies, at a time when family solidarity is extremely important. In Binger's study of twenty-three families, in half the families with previously well siblings, significant behavioral patterns indicated difficulty in coping, with problems such as severe enuresis, headaches, poor school performance, school phobia, depression, severe separation reactions and persistent abdominal pains.[48] Several siblings in this study feared that they, too, might have a fatal disease. They frequently felt guilty and interpreted the parents' preoccupation with the sick child as rejection of themselves.

Solnit and Green found that siblings frequently responded to the sick child's impending death in ways considered inappropriate for adults (but commensurate with the child's developmental level), which upset the parents immensely.[49] In a schema of family-centered nursing care, it would seem important for the nurse to discuss reactions of siblings with the parents, initiating the discussion if the parents do not do so of their own accord. From personal experience, making possible visits of siblings to the sick child in the hospital (regardless or perhaps despite "hospital rules") has helped considerably to clarify many situations and in maintaining family solidarity. In such a situation, however, it becomes imperative for the nurse to be present during the visit, as an observer and interpreter.

A related problem to the dying child in the hospital is what to do when another child on the ward dies. This is usually handled with much evasion and mysterious moving of carts and curtains and beds. Both Yudkin[50] and Vernick and Karon[51] advocate talking truthfully to the children remaining about what happened —even if they do not ask, they know. Vernick and Karon recount a story of tremendous behavioral problems encountered in a nine year old who was to be transferred to another unit. Instead of being told the truth about children who die, he had been told that they were transferred to this particular unit. His behavior was related to the fact that he did not want to go there either, because he knew that children who went there never came back. Again from personal experience, a great deal of anxiety and "behavior difficulty" can be avoided by discussing the situation truthfully with the remaining children on the unit.

The core of the problem of dealing with childrens' perceptions of death and with dying children seems mainly that nurses are human beings, living in a society where death is a hateful and distressing experience and working in a profession which regards death as an enemy. Also, the traditional role of the nurse has been that of assistant to the physician, and involvement in physical activities of care. While physical aspects of care are important, emotional and psychological aspects of the whole family—patient/child and parents and siblings are emerging as equally important. The role of the nurse is changing, too, from one of subservience to one of professional equality. New methods of education and preparation are required to allow the nurse to implement her developing role, especially with regard to the dying child and his family. Both she and the physician must have a greater awareness of their own feelings and therapeutic use of these feelings. In describing the social loss of dying patients, Glaser and Strauss speak of the nurse's traditional response of denial and withdrawal:

> . . . nurses are responding as human beings born into our particular society—a response not necessarily in conflict with professional responses, but not falling within the group of professionally prescribed responses. Nurses import into the hospital the values of our society and act accordingly . . . what surely can be done is to become deliberately aware of the importation so that responses to social loss will not hinder professional requirements for composure and care. If understanding the impact of social loss will help a nurse maintain her composure in the face of dying, she will not be forced to avoid patients whose tragic plight is just too much to take.[52]

And given this understanding, perhaps the nurse can move on to more meaningful intervention for positive resolution of a situation difficult for all involved.

FOOTNOTES

1. Dr. Elisabeth K. Ross, Conference on the Dying Patient (New York, April 19, 1969), College of Physicians and Surgeons.
2. Sylvia Anthony, *The Child's Discovery of Death* (New York, 1940).
3. Paul Schilder and David Wechsler, "The Attitudes of Children Toward Death," *Journal of Genetic Psychology*, 45:1935, pp. 406+.
4. Maria Nagy, "The Child's Theories Concerning Death," *Journal of Genetic Psychology*, 73:1948, pp. 3+.
5. Robert Fulton, in *Explaining Death to Children*, Earl Grollman, ed. (Boston, 1967), pp. 31-32.
6. Simon Yudkin, "Children and Death," *Lancet*, 1:Jan. 7, 1967:38.
7. Robert Kastenbaum, in *Explaining Death to Children*, Earl Grollman, ed. (Boston, 1967) pp. 94-96.
8. Nagy, op.cit., pp. 3-27.
9. James Morrisey, in *Crisis Intervention*, Howard Parad, ed. (New York, 1965), pp. 331.
10. Gregory Rochlin, in *Explaining Death to Children*, Earl Grollman, ed. (Boston, 1967) pp. 51-85.
11. Albert Solnit and Morris Green, "Psychologic Considerations in the Management of Deaths on Pediatric Hospital Services: I," *Pediatrics*, 24:1959:106+.
12. C. M. Binger, et al., "Childhood Leukemia," *New England Journal of Medicine*, Feb. 10, 1969:414+.
13. Joseph Natterson and Alfred G. Knudson, "Observations Concerning Fear of Death in Fatally Ill Children and Their Mothers," *Psychosomatic Medicine*, 22:1960:456+.
14. Nagy, op.cit., p. 7.
15. Ibid., p. 12.
16. Rochlin, op.cit., pp. 57-58.
17. Ibid., pp. 52-53. This brings up an interesting philosophic point in relation to Piaget's intellectual stages, whether or not a 3-5 year old "knows" anything, or the nature of preschool "knowing."
18. Ibid., p. 53.
19. Ibid., pp. 65-66.
20. Ibid., p. 66.
21. Ibid., p. 68.
22. Kastenbaum, op.cit., p. 102.
23. Nagy, op.cit., p. 25.
24. Kastenbaum, op.cit., pp. 103-104.
25. Ibid., p. 104.
26. Ibid., pp. 104-105.
27. Robert Kastenbaum, in *The Meaning of Death*, Herman Feifel, ed. (New York, 1959), p. 112.
28. Ibid., p. 104.
29. Arthur Jersild, *The Psychology of Adolescence* (New York, 1957) p. 157.
30. Yudkin, op.cit., p. 38.
31. Morrisey, op.cit., pp. 324-338.

32. Ibid., p. 334.

33. Albert Solnit and Morris Green, "The Pediatric Management of the Dying Child: II. The Child's Reaction to the Fear of Dying," in *Modern Perspectives in Child Development*, Solnit and Provence, eds., (New York, 1963), p. 227.

34. Albert Solnit, "The Dying Child," *Developmental Medicine and Child Neurology*, 7: 1965: 693.

35. Binger, op.cit., p. 415.

36. George Engel, "Grief and Grieving," *American Journal of Nursing*, 64: 1964: 98.

37. Yudkin, op.cit., p. 39.

38. Ross, op.cit.

39. Yudkin, op.cit., p. 39.

40. Binger, op.cit., p. 415.

41. Joel Vernick and Myron Karon, "Who's Afraid of Death on a Leukemic Ward?" *American Journal of Diseases of Children*, 109:1965: 395.

42. Binger, op.cit., p. 415.

43. Solnit and Green, op.cit., II, p. 222.

44. Yudkin, op.cit., p. 39.

45. Solnit, op.cit., p. 694.

46. Vernick and Karon, op.cit., p. 397.

47. Ibid., p. 396.

48. Binger, op.cit., p. 416.

49. Solnit and Green, op.cit., I, p. 110.

50. Yudkin, op.cit., p. 40.

51. Vernick and Karon, op.cit., p. 394.

52. Barney Glaser and Anselm Strauss, "The Social Loss of Dying Patients," *American Journal of Nursing*, 64: 1964: 121.

BIBLIOGRAPHY

Childrens' Perceptions of Death
Parent/Familial Reaction to Death of a Child

BOOKS:

Anthony, Sylvia, *The Child's Discovery of Death*, New York, Harcourt, Brace & World, Inc., 1940.

Arnstein, Helene, *What to Tell Your Child*, New York, Pocket Books, Inc., 1962.

Blake, Florence, *The Child, His Parent and the Nurse*, Philadelphia, J. B. Lippincott Co., 1954.

Bro, Margueritte H., *When Children Ask*, New York, Harper and Row Publishers, 1940.

Feifel, Herman, ed., *The Meaning of Death*, New York, McGraw-Hill Book Co., 1959.

Ginott, Haim, *Between Parent and Child*, New York, Avon Books, 1969.

Glaser, Barney G., and Anselm L. Strauss, *Awareness of Dying*, Chicago, Aldine Publishing Co., 1965.

Grollman, Earl A., ed., *Explaining Death to Children*, Boston, Beacon Press, 1967.

Gunther, John, *Death Be Not Proud*, New York, Harper and Row, Publishers, 1949.

Hinton, John, *Dying*, Baltimore, Penguin Books, Inc., 1967.

Jersild, Arthur, *The Psychology of Adolescence*, New York, Macmillan Co., 1957.

Kutscher, Austin H., ed., *Death and Bereavement*, New York, Charles C. Thomas, Publisher, 1969.

Marlow, Dorothy R., *Textbook of Pediatric Nursing*, Philadelphia, W.B. Saunders Co., 1965.

Quint, Jeanne C., *The Nurse and the Dying Patient*, New York, Macmillan Co., 1969.

Ross, Elizabeth K., *On Death and Dying*, New York, Macmillan Co., 1969.

Schoenberg, B., Carr, A., & Kutscher, A.H., eds., *Loss and Grief: Psychological Management in Medical Practice*, New York, Columbia University Press, 1970.

Wolf, Ann W. M., *Helping Your Child to Understand Death*, New York, Child Study Association of America, Inc., Revised edition, 1973

ARTICLES IN COLLECTIONS:

Lindemann, Erich, "Symptomatology and Management of Acute Grief," in *Crisis Intervention: Selected Readings,* Howard J. Parad, ed., New York, Family Service Association of America, 1965, pp. 7-21.

Morrissey, James R., "Death Anxiety in Children with Fatal Illness," in *Crisis Intervention: Selected Readings,* Howard J. Parad, ed., Family Service Association of America, New York, 1965, pp. 324-333.

Solnit, Albert J., and Morris Green, "The Pediatric Management of the Dying Child, Part II: The Child's Reaction to Fear of Dying," in *Modern Perspective in Child Development,* Albert J. Solnit and Sally Provence, eds., New York, International Universities Press, Inc., 1963, pp. 217-228.

Jackson, Edgar N., "Helping Children Cope With Death," in *Religion and Bereavement,* Austin H. Kutscher and Lillian G. Kutscher, eds., New York, Health Sciences Publishing Corp., 1972, pp. 161-164.

Jackson, Edgar N., "Understanding the Teenager's Response to Death," Ibid., pp. 147-152.

PERIODICALS:

Baker, Jean M. and Karen C. Sorenson, "A Patient's Concern With Death," *American Journal of Nursing,* vol. 63, no. 7, July, 1963, pp. 90-92.

Binger, C.M., et al., "Childhood Leukemia," *New England Journal of Medicine,* February 28, 1969, pp. 414-418.

Bonine, Gladys, "Students' Reactions to Childrens' Deaths," *American Journal of Nursing,* vol. 67, no. 7, July, 1967, pp. 1439-40.

Bright, Florence, and Sr. Luciana France, "The Nurse and the Terminally Ill Child," *Nursing Outlook,* vol. 15, no. 9, September, 1967, pp. 39-42.

Byers, Mary Lou, "The Hospitalized Adolescent," *Nursing Outlook,* vol. 15, August, 1967, pp. 32-34.

Carpenter, Kathryn M., and Marian J. Stewart, "Parents Take Heart At the City of Hope," *American Journal of Nursing,* vol. 60, no. 10, October, 1962, pp. 82-85.

Editorial, "Death in Childhood," *Canadian Medical Association Journal,* vol. 98, May, 1968, pp. 967-69.

Easson, William M., "Care of the Young Patient Who is Dying," *Journal of the American Medical Association,* vol. 205, no. 4, July 22, 1968, pp. 63-67.

Engel, George L., "Grief and Grieving," *American Journal of Nursing,* vol. 64, no. 9, September, 1964, pp. 93-98.

Erickson, Florence, "Helping the Sick Child Maintain Behavioral Control," *Nursing Clinics of North America*, vol. 2, no. 4, December, 1967, pp. 695-703.

Friedman, Stanford, Paul Chernoff, John Mason and David Hamburg, "Behavioral Observations in Parents Anticipating the Death of a Child," *Pediatrics*, vol. 32, October, 1963, pp. 610-625.

Galiardi, Diane and Margaret S. Miles, "Interactions Between Two Mothers of Children Suffering from Incurable Cancer," *Nursing Clinics of North America*, vol. 4, no. 2, March, 1969, pp. 89-100.

Geis, Dorothy P., "Mothers' Perceptions of Care Given Their Dying Children," *American Journal of Nursing*, vol. 65, no.2, February, 1965, pp. 105-107.

Glaser, Barney and Anselm L. Strauss, "The Social Loss of Dying Patients," *American Journal of Nursing*, vol. 64, no. 6, June, 1964, pp. 119-121.

Gutowski, Frances, "Nursing the Leukemic Child," *American Journal of Nursing*, vol. 63, no. 4, April, 1963, pp. 87-88.

Kneisl, Carol, "Thoughtful Care for the Dying," *American Journal of Nursing*, vol. 68, no. 3, March, 1968, pp. 550-553.

Knudsen, Alfred G. and Joseph Natterson, "Participation of Parents in the Hospital Care of Fatally Ill Children," *Pediatrics*, vol. 26, September, 1960, pp. 482-490.

Levinson, Boris, "The Pet and the Child's Bereavement," *Mental Hygiene*, vol. 5, April, 1967, pp. 197-200.

Meyer, Herbert, "Predictable Problems of Hospitalized Adolescents," *American Journal of Nursing*, vol. 69, no. 3, March, 1969, pp. 525-28.

Murstwin, Bernard, "The Effect of Long Term Illness of Children on the Emotional Adjustment of Parents," *Child Development*, vol. 31, March, 1960, pp. 157-171.

Nagy, Maria, "The Child's Theories Concerning Death," *Journal of Genetic Psychology*, vol. 73, September, 1948, pp. 3-27.

Natterson, Joseph M. and Alfred G. Knudsen, "Observations Concerning Fear of Death in Fatally Ill Children and Their Mothers," *Psychosomatic Medicine*, vol. XXII, no. 6, 1960, pp. 456-465.

Quint, Jeanne C., "Obstacles to Helping the Dying," *American Journal of Nursing*, vol. 66, no.7, July, 1966, pp. 1568-1571.

Schilder, Paul and David Wechsler, "The Attitudes of Children Toward Death," *Journal of Genetic Psychology*, vol. 45, 1955, pp. 406 +.

Sharp, Donna, "Lessons from a Dying Patient," *American Journal of Nursing*, vol. 68, no. 7, July 1968, pp. 1517-1520.

Smith, Ann and Lois Schnieder, "The Dying Child," *Clinical Pediatrics,* vol. 8, no. 3, March, 1969, pp. 131-134.

Solnit, Albert, and Morris Green, "Psychologic Considerations in the Management of Deaths in Pediatric Hospital Services:I," *Pediatrics,* vol. 24, no. 1, July, 1959, pp. 106-112.

Solnit, Albert, "The Dying Child," *Developmental Medicine and Child Neurology,* vol. 7, 1965, pp. 693-695.

Vandenbergh, Richard, "Let's Talk About Death," *American Journal of Nursing,* vol. 66, no. 1, January, 1966, pp. 71-73.

Vernick, Joel and Myron Karon, "Who's Afraid of Death on a Leukemia Ward," *American Journal of Diseases of Children,* vol. 109, May, 1965, pp. 393-397.

Wagner, Bernice, "Teaching Students to Work with the Dying," *American Journal of Nursing,* vol. 64, no. 11, November, 1964, pp. 128-131.

Watson, M. Jean, "Death—A Necessary Concern for Nurses," *Nursing Outlook,* vol. 116, February, 1968, pp. 47-48.

Weinberg, Sheila, Catherine E. Schonberg, and Darlene Y. Grier, "Seminars in Nursing Care of the Adolescent," *Nursing Outlook,* vol. 16, December, 1968, pp. 18-23.

Yudkin, Simon, "Children and Death," *Lancet,* vol. 1, no. 7480, January 7, 1967, pp. 37-41.

Zeligs, Rose, "Death Casts Its Shadow on a Child," *Mental Hygiene,* vol. 5, December, 1967, pp. 9+.

Zeligs, Rose, "Childrens' Attitudes Toward Death," *Mental Hygiene,* Vol. 5, July, 1967, pp. 393-96.

The Dying Child

By Domeena C. Renshaw, M.D.*

When the dying patient is a child, surrounding circumstances seem exceedingly more complex and more painful for all involved. Hard as it is to accept that grown-ups die, we still tend to expect the biblical span of "three score and ten years," and remarks like, "he was so young" when a colleague of forty years dies of a coronary are not uncommon. The expectation of a long span of life makes dealing with predictable death in the really very young a subject so intolerably painful that, as a culture, we tend to deal with it mainly by avoidance. Perhaps underlying is the hope that if we do not look at it it will somehow go away! Or if we just deal with it on the level of improving statistics of infant mortality rates or accelerated growth rates, we can depersonalize it to the point of tolerance.

Most of us manage to function from day to day "as if" we are safe from death and will survive traffic death-tolls and fatal disease. Most of us, too, tend to carry this defense over into our professional dealings with the dying patient, especially the dying child. It is more comfortable for many physicians to go along with parents planning for their 15 year old leukemic son "as if" he were going to graduate from an Ivy League College, than recurrently to deal with the reality of the boy's impending death.

Is this necessarily wrong? Beneath the denial is hope. Hope is a sustaining human quality not to be underestimated in the important role it plays in all goal-directed behavior. Hope of improvement is the motivation behind every dose of medication prescribed. Parent and patient hope that there is an incorrect diagnosis and all will be well. Hope is a real strength in maintaining the will to live. Giving up hope gives place to despair and sorrow.[10,11]

At which point does hope concede to the reality of the inevitable end? The point where with honest professional evaluation, the prognosis for recovery is near zero. At this time we need honestly to confront first and foremost, our own personal feelings, when we, as doctors, have to admit to helplessness before a disease process which is relentless. The entire emphasis and training at every level in medi-

* Clinic Director, Loyola University, Stritch School of Medicine, Department of Psychiatry, 2160 South First Avenue, Maywood, Illinois 60153.

cal school is to combat, avoid and prevent disease and death. When death and disease triumph, some danger exists that medical professionals see this as a personal defeat.[8] Our professional competence too, is challenged. In the rush of a busy day, we may not want to recognize the covered-over feelings of discomfort, perhaps guilt or inadequacy: "Was there something I missed? Should I have asked for another consult? Will the family sue?"

Every medical school teaches students to recognize the signs of death, but how many medical schools offer even one lecture on a doctor's attitude toward dying? Who tells medical students how to break the news of fatal illness to patient and family? Who tells the intern whether he *should* tell and when? Who tells the resident what to expect on giving this information? Who teaches the surgeon and internist to evaluate the strengths and maturity of patient and family so the decision of if, when and how to tell may be made? There is no planned program of training for death. Accidentally, incidentally, or not at all, describes how most doctors learn about the dying period.

We often presume there is a body of knowledge on the topic of dying, and yet there is not. Philosophers and theologians have traditionally been assigned society's task of reflecting on death, but the carry-over is small from the academic to the actual face-to-face behavior and emotions of those of us who deal with the crisis of dying.[4,5,6,7]

Death is an irreversible *state*. Dying is a dynamic *process*, at times reversible, depending on the individual's capacity physically to recover and emotionally to "fight." Thus dying is indeed a *life-task*, a function of the ego or total person, either to rally or to resign. Dying is a crisis in the life of each individual: of return or of separation. Depending on the life-situation of the individual, thoughts of impending separation may be a relief, or bring much pain when there is much joy to lose.

Dying in the child is similar to but not the same as dying in the adult. The older the child, the more developed the ego functions. The younger the child, the less valid it is to "adultomorphise." Experiences and abstract concepts held by the adult may not operate in the child under about 12 years. It must be clearly recognized that concepts about death are phase-related in the child and differ with intellect and precocity.[2,3]

At 2 or 3 years, "dead" may be just a word to a child, without appropriate meaning. By 4 or 5 years he may partially understand

and may think that only animals die, or that death can be caused or reversed by simple wishes, or that only other people die. Up to age 6, 7 or 8 years, the child still has a concept, to a greater or lesser degree, that death is reversible. This is seen in their games, "You're dead, you're alive again"—the statement seems to make the fact. Much in the environment promotes this thinking: television shows the killed or injured again next week; scripture relates how Christ rises from the dead at Easter; reassurance is commonplace by parents that grandmother is happy and well up in Heaven. These are all society's own methods of coping with the thought of death, our own need for immortality.

Around 8 years of age the child becomes interested in *after* death and may pose many difficult questions. The questions are frequently unanswerable other than in context or religious teachings. By age 9 years and over, children are much more able to reason and become quite biological in describing and understanding death. They are prone to describe death as: "stop breathing, no pulse." Usually after 10 years of age, the child is ready for an honest explanation if his own life or that of family members is in danger. His ego strengths are greater, and he is able to mobilize defenses. Secrecy is not a good way to handle the mature latency child. He is aware of what is going on and shows prolonged grief at the loss of loved ones, whether he is the bereaved, or himself in the process of dying.

Narcissism is a common human quality. With growth and socialization we are taught to handle our expectations of immediate gratification by considering others, by reducing our demands, by tolerating frustration. This is a slow learning process which breaks down under stresses, such as anxiety caused by our own illness or the loss of loved ones. The younger the child, the newer the learning and the more rapid the regression to earlier behavior of primary narcissism, such as crying, clinging, demanding to be held, feeling abandoned when mother leaves, and immediate comfort when she returns.

Anxiety in the sick child may show in regression to earlier behavior, such as bedwetting, thumbsucking, rocking, temper tantrums and fluffy toy clinging. Staff should not forget that the hospital represents unfamiliar surroundings and strange people to the child. The dying child may whimper, not because he is "afraid of death," but rather because of temporary loss of his important love object—mother. Or maybe he is upset by the loss of a function such as bladder or bowel control; or of speech in a tracheostomy, or of motor power with certain drugs. Recognize and verbalize for the child these very real fears, discuss the loss of function to reduce his feelings of shame, terror or isolation. Tell him you understand he is upset, give the time of mother's next visit. Wherever possible, in the terminal phases of the illness, give unrestricted visiting privileges to close family members.[12]

"Should the child be told?" is a question that may come up when the end is near. Many times parents will ask the doctor not to tell the child, thinking they may protect him from their own pain of knowing the truth. The doctor may, with unconscious relief, go along with this. But since the doctor's first duty is to his patient, it is his task to evaluate whether it is in the best interest of the patient to be given honest information about his condition, how much information and when? To burden a child with knowledge that he is unable conceptually to integrate into his thinking would be of no particular value other than to initiate an immediate fear of the unknown, e.g., to tell a 3-year-old "You are going to die" might be equivalent to telling him he is to be given a "shot" and his reaction may be similar. To tell this child he is very sick is both truthful, more understandable, and useful in obtaining co-operation in nursing and care procedures.

However to go along with massive family denial to a teenage leukemic girl who is a cheer-leader, or a puberty boy with sarcoma bent on continuing in Little League, is hardly fair to the child. The question of how much to say, and how soon, is difficult and can not be generalized. Careful consideration of the coping devices of each parent adds further complexity. Each case is different, and there are no pat answers. Lying is a mistake. When discovered by the patient, he is left confused, angry, insecure and alone—all of which could have been prevented. An active teenager with newly diagnosed leukemia can handle certain information: that he has a problem with his blood and needs regular medication and follow-up, that he may feel some weakness, which he should recognize in order to put some limitations of his own on his activities. Preferably such a talk should be given with both parents present, both for reinforcement for the parents (who frequently in the early stages, seeing the child well, may deny the illness) and to eliminate pathological secrets in the family.[7]

Should the parents be given the diagnosis when made? Again, this depends on parents: what the word means to them and how they will be able to handle the information. If the course is fluctuating and sometimes long, as in leukemia, this should be stated clearly, together with the seriousness and fatality. People are known to hear what they want to hear, and one hopeful statement is often selected out of all the rest. So it is not surprising when families function "as if" the child is normal. Nor is this necessarily wrong. As stated before, dying is a *life*-task, and for some the choice is to live out the terminal time as fully and normally as possible. Whether this is a mature choice or denial on the part of family and patient, the main criterion for the doctor to evaluate is whether the *patient* is comfortable this way. If the patient is under excess pressure and strain to please a parent by continuing the "game" of denial and pretense, the doctor should intervene and allow the patient some relief. The tension caused by such denial and avoidance puts distance between child and family and can be painfully isolating to the patient. Honest revelation of his illness allows the suppressed sorrow to surface. There is relief in crying, expression of regret, and security in the closeness that comes from the awareness that he is *loved*.

This relief and security can be expected to alternate with anxiety about the impending separation and the unknown of dying and death. The anxiety may be conscious and expressed, or go unrecognized if defenses such as denial and reaction-formation are operating in the child and those around him. Anxiety may be expressed as irritability. There may be projection of anger onto loved ones or nursing staff, making the task of service to the dying child exceptionally difficult, since the counter-aggression mobilized in staff by the "bitchy" dying child creates much guilt in staff, particularly if they do not understand the mechanisms. They tend to reject and avoid him as much as possible. Isolation results, which is frightening to the child, and which increases the anxiety in a vicious circle. Staff needs to verbalize for the parents' and patient's recognition of underlying emotions: "You're upset and angry" and then understanding and sympathy, "We know this is very hard for you," and wherever possible, praise for endurance, "You're doing a fine job."

A mature death is rare, even in the aged. Preparedness, acceptance and the capacity to separate without anger or yearning to remain are not easy. The task of dying frequently evokes regression in the personality. Whining, crying, demanding behavior, clinging, explosive angry tantrums, rocking, feeling abandoned in the presence of family, should be anticipated by staff, who are then able to assist the family by understanding the patient's great need at this time for closeness. "He is not angry, he is frightened. Just hold his hand and tell him you will stay with him." Usually comfort and support emotionally are supplied by the presence of familiar loved ones and assist both the patient and his family. The patient's sense of isolation is reduced. Death is a solitary life-task in the end. It is in the time *before the end* that closeness of loved ones is significant. That is why we allow extended visiting privileges when patients are on danger lists.

Dying is also a time of preliminary mourning, both for the dying child and parent or family member. John Bowlby[1] described with great clarity the three stages of mourning observable as early as age 15 months:

I. Protest—anger, hope clinging.

II. Despair—hope relinquished, tears, depression.

III. Detachment—uninterested.

The same reactions are noted in "temporary mourning." When the child is hospitalized and "loses" mother, even temporarily, he may entertain a fantasy of permanent loss. Depending on the child, stages may be skipped, and all staff know the "stony" detached, fatally ill child, who refuses to react. Parents show phases of mourning too as they hold their vigil at the deathbed. Some may try to be "strong" and show hope and cheerfulness, trying to deny the reality. Their mourning is delayed—if they repress, the task of mourning will be theirs at a later date. Many parents are seen in Stage I: protest, anger at staff, even at the child, in their own sorrow. In the less defended, grieving despair is seen early. For most this despair comes usually when death is pronounced, although some mothers may come a year later to psychiatrists saying, "I just couldn't cry, I froze up, I was numb at the funeral." Delayed sorrow may then emerge, allowing the final task of mourning, namely, acceptance and integration, to occur.

The hospital is frequently the setting for the terminal process, so the question of how professional staff handles the dying child becomes increasingly important.[9] Energy is mobilized towards helping the chronically ill child and his family cope and adapt to the disability. This is active and easy, and morale is high with much hope that science will soon come up with a cure. However, there is a strange shift as termination sets in. Some experienced nurses say they can "smell death." At this time they will attempt to isolate the child by drawing curtains, using a private room or a "death bed" often close to the nursing station. Usually this means hope has been given up. Intensive Care may become an alternative, with the child being removed from the ward. Dealing with family may then be by personnel totally unfamiliar with the case.

Questions arise such as: Who should tell parents? If there is a private physician, usually the task is clearly his. However, many residents and interns have handled this responsibility for attending men. For staff patients there are no clear-cut rules to guide. The Danger-List is one medium devised, perhaps, to help depersonalize the first impact. Often the news is given to family by a charge-nurse, sometimes new to parents and child, where for the new nurse the pain is less because she has less personal involvement. We all know how frequently feelings get involved in the desperate attempt to save the dying child, resulting in anger between nurse and doctor about management; blame for omissions and commissions; ambivalence and turmoil at who turns off the respirator and when; or should there have been resuscitation or why was it done?[8] The discomfort of living without the answers is as great for staff as it is for patient and family.

There are no absolutes, no protocols and no guidelines. Each case is unique and needs careful consideration, understanding, and compassionate handling by staff. Listen to the parents' desperate questions, tolerate their frenzied attempts to get more powerful help. Understand their wanting to cling to hope since they cannot tolerate the anxiety at the impending loss of their child. Perhaps they have guilt at not having done more, or being the cause of the illness or for feeling relieved that death is impending since they may have financial stress. So many complex factors operate at this time that verbal content alone is misleading. Just let them express their feelings. Do not try to stop the tears and the grief (unless grossly excessive) for these are appropriate at this point of crisis and healthier than stony, numb suppression. Grief and mourning are essential components of working through important losses, and if repressed or heavily tranquilized the important maturational impact on the personality is lost. Catastrophe and crisis can be for many important times of growth and learning.[4]

Traditionally the para-death time has been the realm of priest, minister, rabbi. Although increasingly hospital charts read "Religion—none," staff should still ask the family whether they might want to have their chaplain attend.

For staff, the business aspect of death certificates, statistics, autopsy, other forms, and informing appropriate personnel makes this period busy and more bearable. Perhaps the task of complex funeral arrangements do much the same for the family and should not be minimized in therapeutic value as final expressions of love, sorrow or expiation.[7] Social workers should resist the impulse to "take over" for the over-whelmed family. It is more useful in the eventual resolution of the grief to assist the bereaved parents to handle details themselves, giving only informational assistance. A couple may be brought closer together and may support each other emotionally in a way they may not have achieved otherwise.

What about the post-death depression on the unit, noticeable in staff, other parents and some little patients, who may plaintively ask for the dead child? The tendency is usually to deny and avoid such feelings. Phrases such as, "She's better off now," "all for the best," are common clichés at such times in attempted rationalization and solace for ourselves and others. Appropriate expressions of mature regret, frustration and sense of loss are also in order, should be recognized, tolerated, even welcomed.

Our knowledge and observations should be accumulated, evaluated and recorded in a form available and useful to colleagues present and future. The more we discuss and handle this topic, the more understandable and manageable this final life-period of the child should become for all involved.

BIBLIOGRAPHY

1. Bowlby, John: Childhood mourning. International Journal of Psychoanalysis of the Child. December, 1961.
2. Gesell Institutes' Child Behavior, Ilg & Ames, Dell Publishing Company.
3. Gartley,W., and Betnasconi, M.: The concept of death in children. J. Genet. Psychol. 1967, 110/1 (71-85).
4. Gorer, G.: *Death, Grief and Mourning.* London, Cresset Press, 1965.
5. Hinton, J.: *Dying.* Penquin Books, 1967.
6. Marks, R. K.: Dying. Medical Proceedings, October 19, 1968.
7. Mitford, Jessica: *The American Way of Death.* London, Hutchinson, 1963.
8. Quint, Jeanne C.: *The Nurse and the Dying Patient.* New York, Macmillan, 1967.
9. Saunders, Cicely: *The Management of Terminal Illness.* London, Hospital Medical Publications Ltd., 1967.
10. Wahl, C. W.: The fear of death. Bull. Menninger Clinic 22:214-223, November, 1958.
11. Wahl, C. W.: Bolstering the defenses of the dying patient. Hospital Physician, March, 1969.
12. Wald, F. S.: To everything there is a season and a time to every purpose. The New Physician, April, 1969.

Paper reprinted by permission of the *Archives of the Foundation of Thanatology*, Vol. 2, No. 4, Winter, 1970.

Grief and the Young: A Need to Know

*Karl O. Budmen, Ph.D.**

It is probable that in the years between kindergarten and high s‹
graduation, most students will have some experience with death, grief,
bereavement. Not uncommon is the loss of a parent, a loved one, a re‹
teacher or some other pivotal adult, even a classmate. Confronted by d
our young often find themselves very much alone. Neither their peers
the adults around them know quite what to say, what to expect, what to
how to spare unnecessary pain or give needed assistance and support. I
their teachers, whose expertise is the area of growth and development
whose function is nurturing, are uncertain and unsure in their efforts to

If death shocks us by reminding us of our own mortality, bereaver
embarrasses us by underscoring our helplessness in the face of grief. I
is even an irony in that helplessness. Schools which can prepare stud
for college, develop marketable vocational skills, make honest efforts at cit
ship training, preparation for home and family living, health instruction,
education, worthy use of leisure—in short, which can try to educate for li
are yet impotent in dealing with that most human of life processes — deatl

Such neglect, born as it is of lack of insight and fear, is neither nece‹
nor excusable. If we can predict patterns of human growth from birt]
death and can identify norms for specific periods of development, surely
can use comparable approaches to gain understanding and knowledge of hu
reactions to death. Grief and bereavement are, above all, *human* condition
normal, understandable, predictable. Helping young people to cope
these is the responsibility of all who serve youth, not merely the sp‹
domain of physicians and clergy.

What is needed is an on-going dialogue among those concerned
youth and the problems of grief and bereavement — teachers, school ad
istrators, social workers, clergy, physicians, psychologists — all who can l
and help through such dialogue. Some participants may be already knowle
able and there is a need for them to share that knowledge. Others can b
that special perspective which their particular background, experience,
training provide.

Beyond its educative function, however, such dialogue may expose a
in which our knowledge is limited or missing and give impetus to the rese‹
needed for obtaining that knowledge. It is entirely possible that the f‹
and design of such research may be worked out in the course of t]
deliberations.

---

* Professor of Education, State University College, New Paltz, New York.

Research is our other desperate need. Presently our reaction to the grief-
ken is more well-intentioned than well-informed. Physicians can prescribe
quilizers, but they are not sure they should. Concerned clergy, educators,
sympathetic friends can attempt consolation, but they are often at a loss
ffer anything more constructive. Psychiatrists can recognize differences in
needs of bereaved children, adolescents, and adults, but have few norms
vhich to assess individual behavior.

Clearly *we have a need to know.* We can begin by recognizing that
is not a dybbuk to be exorcised, but a process to be understood. It is
ous that the process is more than physical, more than psychological, more
spiritual, more than social — indeed, no less than human. Its very dimen-
requires that its study be equally broad. The Foundation of Thanatology
ngularly suited to provide that focus and to undertake that challenge.

A Look at Death in Children's Poetry

By Stuart Milstein*

As a poetry consultant in the elementary schools, in New York City, I worked with students ranging in age from seven to twelve (grades two-six). Most of them came from middle class families and were of average intelligence. My job was to "teach" them how to write poetry. (You can't teach writing, you can only provoke it.) Working with a class for an hour a week during a period of four weeks I tried to lure, trick and even shock the kids away from the rational approach towards writing. I did this by giving them writing assignments which often required that they react irrationally, imaginatively, or "poetically." Most of them quickly realized that they were not expected to write a neatly organized composition about their dog or their summer vacation. Many opened themselves up and wrote highly charged, emotional and insightful poems and prose pieces.

Generally the topics chosen allowed the children to compensate for their lack of strength in a world run by big people. They were asked to pretend that they were shamans, witches, magicians, God, gods, and to write about what they would do. For example:

If I were God I'd create a Father Nature. (Grade 3)

If I were a witch I would take all the people to Mars and I would have the earth all to myself. I would make a magic poison that turns people into dogs. I would take away all the things people like and give them what they hate. If I were a good witch I would give all the children playgrounds and toys. I would give the men and women money. I would sometimes turn myself into a princess and help other people.

If I could make any kind of magic poison some would be healthy and some would be bad.

If I were a witch I would be good and bad. (Grade 3)

But I also assigned other topics which required them to pretend that they were animals, plants or inanimate objects. In these

---

* Stuart Milstein teaches in the New York City School system.

assignments the older students especially sometimes revealed tremendous doubts about themselves. They were starting to commit themselves, emotionally, at least in their poems.

> *A piece of dust is floating and hardly ever stops. This is what I used to be. Its life is just ease and doesn't really amount to anything.*
>
> *Then, all of a sudden, a bright yellow sunbeam came and pow! I never knew what hit me. Now I am disintegrated. (Grade 5)*

The responses were encouraging. Once the children were used to being allowed to express their feelings of being omnipotent, magical or able to change their shapes, I gave them exercises which were more challenging, closer to home but awesome, emotionally charged. I asked them to describe death, to speak with the dead and to have the dead speak through them. In assignments that progressively brought them closer to the present I asked them to use their powers to communicate with dead presidents, baseball stars, cherished pets, relatives, grandparents, parents, brothers, sisters—the response was incredible. The writing was evocative and sad or funny (sometimes both). It covered the widest possible emotional range of reactions to the tragedy of death.

> *Death is like a long plane ride when the plane is shot down and you start to walk for 1000 miles. (Grade 5)*
>
> *Death is the end of a line of cement. (Grade 5)*
>
> *Death is like the last word of a song. (Grade 5)*
>
> *Death is like a broken record. (Grade 5)*

For some, death did not seem very frightening. They would summon up a dead relative to speak with him and end by being flippant or inappropriately practical.

> *Oh! Uncle Harry, I hope you are alright. Please be. I hear you talking through me. Speak. Down in Hell or up in Heaven. Is G-d feeding you? Grow nice and fat. Not skinny like my brother. (Grade 2)*

Oh Grandpa, please come up from your grave.
I can't. I can't get a subway. Anyway if I did, people would
be scared of me.
No one is going to be scared of you, Gramp.
This coffin is better than my bed, and I don't have to wake
up so early. . . . (Grade 4)

Some of them were less flippant but still not very frightened by
death. One might call them "optimists."

Grandmother, it is nice to speak to you again, and I love you
so much.
So do I my child, love you so much.
Grandmother, tell me how you are doing?
I'm doing fine. People are nice to me. I take barefoot walks
on the clouds.
I'm glad you are getting exercise. Goodbye, I love you grand-
mother. (Grade 4)

Oh grandpa, it's me, your granddaughter. Talk to me, please.
I hear you. What do you want?
What are you doing, Grandpa?
I'm playing with angels.
Grandpa, well, I'm on earth and it's nice. (Grade 2)

As I said above not all the writing was lighthearted. For some
children, summoning up the dead proved to be a painful process.

I wish that I can talk to my grandpa. He is dead now.
I want to talk to my grandpa now. I miss him.
I want to see him now, mother.
(I miss him very much. How come he is dead now?)
I can never see him now.
I want to see him now, now, now.
Mother, I can see him in make-believe.
Here. Grandpa, where are you now? (Grade 2)

I would like my baby sister to come back.
Baby, baby baby sister, where have you been?
I am dead. Don't you see?
We need you. I don't like you because you are dead, baby
baby sister. . . (Grade 2)

For other children, death was neither approachable nor understandable. Perhaps it was because there had recently been a death in the family, or maybe death, to them, was always something ominous. Below is a poem by a child who envisions death as a horror—a cannibalistic witch doctor.

I am crying. The witch doctor killed my grandpa and I am crying. I do not like the witch doctor.
The witch doctor is talking tonight. A witch doctor is not good. A witch doctor is bad.
The witch doctor talks and cries.
Mrs. Witchdoctor and Mr. Witchdoctor are talking tonight.
I am talking and crying.
They will eat me up, they cry. (Grade 2)

There were other children who were also frightened by death (it was ominous for them, too) but they prayed. Sometimes the prayers were offered to God and sometimes they were like wishes transcribed from their stream-of-consciousness.

If me, my mother, my father, my brother, all my friends, all my relatives, all the people that I love, if they could only live forever, it would be so good I would never have to cry and I wouldn't have to go to any funerals, or graveyards, and see graves with people I love very, very much lying there wishing they were alive. . . . (Grade 4)

When rereading these works, I have had to remind myself that children wrote them, because of the range and depth of their reactions to death. Here are jokers, optimists, pessimists; those who play, those who pray, and those who fear. Their reactions seem to have little to do with their intelligence and no more to do with their grade level than their vocabulary level. Their reactions seem to come from the bedrock of their experience, ultimately revealing how they understand and relate to mortality. They are full of the same rituals, games, and fears that many grownups are. Writing poetry based on these feelings seems an especially effective tool for helping children reach, understand and deal with their conceptions of death.

In a graveyard my uncle said from his grave: "when you are dead it is like being in a dark, dark tunnel with no end." In Heaven my uncle said: "Heaven is like being in a wonderland of stars." (Grade 5)

On Death

By Barbara Multer*

It is important to discuss death. It is important to be able to discuss death with the family and the dying person and to help each one of the family to cope with his grief. But it is wrong and impossible to attempt to absolve the grief of the dying man. Taking away his grief is tantamount to saying that his life was simply not worth living. Why should a man "cope" with his grief? It is his right to grieve and it is only right that he do so. It is his final affirmation that his life, to him at least, has been worthwhile and that he is sorry to leave it.

I believe that the focus of the present interest in death is wrong. Nothing can be done for a dying man who has lived "like a corpse;" it is not his death that matters but his life. There is no way to comfort a seventeen-year-old who is going to die. There is nothing one can say to absolve the horrible, bitter injustice of it.

I think that the focus should be shifted to the surviving relatives who must live without a loved one. It is impossible to comfort a dying man unless, of course, he believes that he is going on to something better. But chances are that if he believes this, he has wasted his life in the rigid "corpse"—like morality or religion—and must believe in a heavenly afterlife as justification for his empty life.

It must be faced. Death is agonizing. Death is sad and terrible in every case, in every way. It is also inevitable and unless we learn to accept that and live every moment to its fullest, we are cheating ourselves out of much precious time from the only certain thing we are given at birth: our lives.

How I die makes little difference to me. Of course, I wish that it will be as painless and as fast as possible but that essentially makes no difference. It is how I live that matters. If there is any heaven, it is here on earth and it is the same of hell. We make our own mixtures of the two.

---

* Barbara Multer is a high school student in Scarsdale, N.Y.

When I am dying, I shall grieve tremendously. But if I am lucky, it will be because my life really meant something to me. As Camus once said of the Algerians, whom he admired very much, "I have seen two of them die. They were full of horror but silent."

And finally, at the very moment of my death, when I am beyond the power to grieve or hope, I wish mine will be a "happy death" as Camus describes it. I hope the knowledge that my life was lived as I wanted it to be captures the moment.

As Mersault says in the last passage of Camus' *The Stranger*:

And I, too, felt ready to start life all over again. It was as if that great rush of anger had washed me clean, emptied me of hope, and gazing up at the dark sky spangled with its signs and stars, for the first time, the first, I laid my heart open to the benign indifference of the universe. To feel it so like myself, indeed, so brotherly, made me realize that I'd been happy, and that I was happy still.

Understanding the Teenager's Response to Death

By Edgar N. Jackson, D.D.

There was a time when it was assumed that adolescence was the best part of life. The teen-ager was considered to be free of the obligations of maturity and yet mature enough to enjoy life and its pleasures. Now these assumptions have been largely abandoned. Much of the evidence shows that the period from the end of child-hood to the beginning of adulthood is filled with social, psychological and emotional stress, and that our youth are having serious difficulties in moving through this period of life.

Part of the problem, at least, emerges at the point where the young face the meaning of life and death; when they try to come to terms with their own existence. Contemporary youth, born since the end of World War II, have been the first generation to feel the full brunt of the death-denying, death-defying concept of life that modern man adopted to help him escape the brutality, the suffering, and the death-centeredness of the war-time period. The implication was that if we denied war, it might go away, and if we did not face the meaning of nuclear devices, their destructiveness might never never be un-leashed upon us. No matter how irrational and fanciful such attitudes may be, there has been little restraint on such modes of thought, and the group chiefly affected is our young people who have never known any other way of thinking.

Certainly, one aspect of what Geoffrey Gorer calls the "pornography of death" has been especially directed toward our children and youth. The flooding of the minds of children and youth with the comic-book version of brutality, sadism and apparently meaningless killing has long been a matter of concern. Frederic Wertham's book *Seduction of the Innocent* has made people aware of the problem of this type of informal and indiscreet education. But few seem to realize that this is but a part of the larger pattern of our culture that treats both life and death as trivial, without depth or purpose, and, at best, as intrusions on the thrills and sensational pursuits of the moment.

An unrealistic approach to death can be a hazard to adolescents as they face the major and significant tasks of this period of their lives

In a recent book Avery Weisman, writing on the relation of responsibility to the sense of reality, says quite emphatically, "In short, to be responsible, man must believe in his own death." How difficult it is, then, for our teenagers to develop this form of responsibility, when the culture in which they are growing up works so hard to deny it.

This difficulty shows up at three points. The youth in any culture is faced with three major decisions: He is expected to lay the foundations for a philosophy of life; he is faced with the tasks of sexual adjustment that lead to the choice of a life partner; and he is expected to choose a vocation. In some cultures there is enough social structure to aid in making these choices, but in ours it is a complicated process with few fixed points of reference. It can be shown that the person's attitude toward death may in many cases be a significant factor in determining behavior in relation to these major choices.

Because a philosophy of life is basic to vocational choice and marriage attitudes, let us look at this first. The philosophy of life one develops may vary from time to time in response to one's life experience. Yet the meaning of life to the individual who is living it is a basic ingredient. And the meaning for the individual life is related to the attitudes toward life and death that are prevalent in the social context. The youth growing up in any given era is bound to be affected by that era, for good or ill.

The generation of youth now struggling to create a philosophy of life must contend with contemporary sources of anxiety, the prevalent concept of the future, and the impact of a death-denying, death-defying culture. While it is almost universal for teenagers to express some of their feelings for independence in revolt against their parents, adults like to feel that the future is in the hands of oncoming generations and that they can in some measure control it by their guidance. But in our time, youth is increasingly excluded from an orderly approach to the future, and the value structure that many adults live by seems to be seriously threatened by a whole generation of youth who see life and the world quite differently. Why is this so?

The teenager in our culture is largely a misfit. He has no active social function and no significant economic life. He is ostensibly preparing for a future that he does not define and is spending money that he does not earn. There are few jobs for teenagers, and our culture, with so much learning to transmit, must keep him in school for a long period of time. Even when he has finished his schooling, his future is uncertain because of the military needs of his society. All of this external experience is organized within a highly sensitive and carefully trained individual who draws his own philosophical conclusions. Often this leads him to a feeling of meaninglessness for the processes of life in which he is engaged, and causes him to face the future with apprehension and the present with various types of revolt.

Because the future is always related to concepts of life and death, he takes the anxiety that he has been steeped in, and the meaninglessness of the future which he has developed, and builds types of behavior that are expressions of both. He tends to focus his attention more and more on the present and on the satisfaction of his immediate needs. Increasingly, this becomes gratification without relatedness. As Gorer has shown, this leads to a breakdown of those refined capacities for genuine relationship that can bring meaning to life and that have always been the characteristics of the more truly mature and fulfilled human being.

These qualities of mind and emotion underlie the attitudes of youth toward death and dying. This process is surrounded by denials which make death something that only happens to other people. The emotions that are expressed at the breaking of relationships through death are apt to be of a foreign nature. This makes the traditional sentiments seem irrelevant and inappropriate. In their place are substituted games and other activities that show disregard for life, in an effort to show control over the anxiety about death. Such games as "chicken" illustrate this, as well as the suicidal activities examined in Abt's "Acting Out."

It is but a short step for the youth to direct his inherent idealism and his inherited apprehension toward the focal point of his anxiety. The meaninglessness of the future is equated with the meaninglessness of life and death. In this mood, anything that reminds him of the inevitable but threatening evidence of man's mortal nature is discredited or denied. Thus the significant therapeutic resources developed by society for meeting the emotional crises incident to death are apt to be ridiculed and destroyed.

On the other hand, these same forces at work in personality may become unconscious determinants in vocational choice. I have interviewed a large number of students in professional schools, and have had access to projective tests evaluating their emotional drives. I have found that in a significant number of instances the selection of a vocation was a form of behavior aimed at discovering answers about the meaning of life and death. This appeared to be especially true of clergymen, physicians, research psychologists, psychiatrists, and funeral directors. Perhaps this is one of the explanations for the dichotomy we see in modern society concerning death; the general community tends to ignore or deny the fact of death, whereas careful researchers in the field of human behavior give increasing consideration to the importance of death and a responsible approach to it as basic to maturity and to a sense of responsibility.

The same factors are at work in regard to the choice of a life partner. If the future is important and life perspectives are formed on the basis of an adequate philosophy of life, then marriage will be important and the selection of a partner will be seriously considered. On the other hand, if the future is nebulous and largely irrelevant to life, both the serious approach to the future and the ethical framework for such a future are discounted. This in turn leads to irresponsible sexual behavior and a further breakdown in the institution of marriage and the stability of the society of which it is an important part.

If we look carefully at the statistics on population, we see that today about half of the population in our country is 25 years of age or younger. This means that in our rapidly changing culture an increasingly large amount of the decision-making responsibilities will be in the hands of our youth. If they allow the prevalent patterns of culture to dominate their thinking and action, they will be increasingly death-denying and death-defying. But if they can be made aware of significant research findings on human behavior relating to death and a philosophy of life large enough to compass all of life experience, they will be responsive to those concerns which would adequately provide for the acute emotional crises of life, socially and psychologically.

It is quite obvious that the young people growing up in such rapidly changing times will not be satisfied with the answers of the past, which depended largely on tradition and unexamined premises. They will want to know why things are done as they are, what the values are in the old ways of doing things, and what the significance is for them in the rites, rituals, and ceremonials that they have inherited. That they will be responsive to answers to the personality sciences can be assumed, whereas they would show little response to the appeals of tradition and sentiment.

These young people will have grown up in the most affluent society in human history. They have been so saturated with things, that acquisition in and of itself does not impress them as much as it did their parents. They are more interested in services. They spend more and more on recreation, personal satisfaction, and their needs as individuals. Appeals on the basis of things like quality merchandise will make little response, but satisfactions on the basis of personal services will be valued. Thus, if the significant resources of our culture for meeting emotional crises are to be preserved during this era of rapid change, it will be done through an appeal to the values of those who represent the future. The values of our youth grow from a concern about their inner being, their feelings, and their apprehensions. If they can be understood and met at the level where they make their judgments, they can preserve the practices of the present for even more significant reasons than the present generation employs. If, however, the therapeutic resources which have been developed through the centuries to sustain life in crises are not interpreted to our youth primarily in terms of sentiment and tradition, material value, and social custom, they will be summarily rejected.

Whether we can move into the future with strengthened concepts of family living, significant motivations for vocation, and responsible and mature philosophies of life, may depend more than we realize on facing the personal and social problems that emerge at a point where we make it possible for our youth to confront the relevance of life to death, and of death to life.

HOW ADULTS REACT TO THE SICK, DYING, OR BEREAVED CHILD

Shielding From Awareness: An Aspect of Family Adaptation to Fatal Illness in Children

Edward H. Futterman, M.D.[*] and Irwin Hoffman[**]

In the course of our work with more than thirty families with leukemic children we have conceptualized family coping in relation to a series of adaptational tasks.[1, 2] One such task involves management of awareness of the illness among family members.

We have been impressed by the tendency of most parents to hold tenaciously to the belief that their children regardless of age, are oblivious to the fatal prognosis of leukemia. Many parents actively shield the sick child and his siblings from awareness of the terminal nature of the disease, arguing that such information would cause the children damaging and unnecessary anxiety. The same parents, however, contend that notions of death and dying are beyond their children's comprehension, thereby rendering "leaks" of information innocuous.

Such beliefs in the ignorance of children are contradicted by our interviews and observations. Exposure of children to discussions about leukemia between doctor and parents and among parents is extensive. It is common for parents and doctors to talk over the children's heads concerning the child's chances of survival and the parents' reactions of anxiety and grief. One mother in the presence of her leukemic child, remarked, "We never talk about it in front of him." When a social worker suggested, "But you are now!", mother blandly rejoined, "Oh no, I never do."

Such perceptual screening and selectivity go hand in hand with biased interpretations by parents of what they hear from the children themselves. For example, one mother had a discussion with the 6-year-old sibling of a fatally ill child in which he asked about the child's illness and medication. He pressed his mother by inquiring "What will happen to Roger after they run out of medications?" Mother replied, "He will go to heaven." The sibling responded perfunctorily, "Oh, okay!" seeming satisfied and abruptly changing the subject.

[*] Assistant Professor of Psychiatry, Director of Child Psychiatry, University of Illinois College of Medicine, Chicago, Illinois.

[**] Instructor in Psychology, University of Illinois College of Medicine, Chicago, Illinois.

Mother reported this as evidence that the child had not felt awareness of his sibling's anticipated death.

Siblings also reveal much greater awareness in the sick children than is ascribed to them by the parents. One sibling reported his 4-year-old brother's often saying "I gonna die." In addition, supposedly unaware siblings have accurately described the child's illness as well as its prognosis.

Another family of a 12-year-old girl who died of leukemia insisted that she was unaware of her illness until the end. These parents told of a fund drive for leukemia to which the daughter reacted by quipping, "Why don't they just collect me?"

For the most part we have respected each family's strategy for managing awareness, despite the apparent inconsistencies. However, we have become increasingly concerned about the isolating effect of the myth that children are ignorant of the implications of the illness, a myth which apparently protects the parents more than it does the child. We have also become aware of our own complicity in the perpetuation of the myth. While recognizing the delicate adaptational equilibrium which families coping with leukemia must maintain over a long period of time, we have become convinced of the need to risk upsetting the balance by challenging the notion that children are too young to understand and by working to bring into the open their anxieties and fantasies about death and dying.

1. Futterman, E. H. and Hoffman, I., Crisis of Confidence (in preparation).

2. Sabshin, M., Futterman, E. H. and Hoffman, I., Empirical Studies of Healthy Adaptation (in preparation).

Child Psychiatry Clinic
Neuropsychiatric Institute
University of Illinois

This article was reprinted from the *Archives of the Foundation of Thanatology*, Vol. II, No. 1, Copyright © 1970 by the Foundation of Thanatology.

The Mother and Her Sick Newborn Child

Diller B. Groff, M.D.*

Although the healthy newborn baby is largely a stranger (even though he has been known after a fashion by his new family for nine months), he immediately starts to interact with his mother and begins his integration into the family constellation from the moment of birth. But what about the newborn with a life-threatening congenital abnormality? Modern medical management usually requires the immediate transfer of the sick newborn to an intensive care unit, perhaps in another hospital, where he is removed from the mother by several glass panels, surrounded by complex equipment and tended by many skilled personnel. Often the mother is not allowed to interact in any way with the child while he is in an intensive care unit.

If such a sick newborn dies in these first weeks of life, the mother may have seen him only for a few minutes at the time of birth or for a few hours after delivery. The mother in such circumstances with pre-delivery sedation and analgesia plus the rigors of delivery may not accept the reality of her child's birth and death. Without being able to hold, caress and care for her sick infant, she may resort to fantasies about the child and the events concerning her pregnancy and delivery with possible damage to her own personality and to her relationship with the remaining family.

To prevent such fantasies, many physicians now encourage the mother to participate as much as possible in the care of the sick newborn, even if this is only touching and caressing the infant through the ports of an isolette. Then the reality of the life she has planned for over the past nine months is manifest, the mother has an opportunity to express her love for her baby and, while the death of the infant may be immediately more distressing, the mother will later better understand and accept the death.

There may be resistance by the nursing staff to this participation by the mother in the care of the sick baby, a role which many nurses feel is theirs alone. The mother herself may be fearful and uncertain that she belongs with the sick infant. The nurses' resistance can be overcome by teaching them the rationale for allowing the mother to

* Chief, Pediatric Surgery, Catholic Medical Center of Brooklyn & Queens, Inc.

be with the infant. The physician must take time to listen to the mother's questions and give her support in working through her fears and anxieties concerning her sick child. The physician must not shirk this task even though it is often more difficult than the care of the baby.

Catholic Medical Center of Brooklyn and Queens, Inc.
88-25 153rd Street
Jamaica, New York 11432

This article was reprinted from the *Archives of the Foundation of Thanatology*, Vol. II, No. 2, Copyright © 1970 by the Foundation of Thanatology.

The Pediatrician and the Dying Child

*Mary E. Robinson, Ph.D.**

All physicians are dedicated to the preservation of life, but nature is on the side of the pediatrician. Once his patients have survived the ordeal of birth (when they are largely the responsibility of the obstetrician) and the moderately hazardous first months of life, it is unlikely that while in "the pediatric years" they will die. Unlike surgeons, internists and cardiologists, the young pediatrician may practice for some time without a single patient death. Thus when a patient does die, he may have had little experience in dealing with the situation.

The pediatrician also has a problem peculiar to his specialty: each patient represents at least two, possibly three and sometimes more people with whom he must deal—the child, the mother, the father and, on occasion, the doting grandparents. Should the child die, he must cope with the feelings of all these people.

Like all physicians, the pediatrician is only human. His practice makes incredible demands on his time and energy, leaving little of either for involvement with the dying child and his family. The imminent death of a patient brings an uncomfortable awareness of his own fears about dying and, if he is a parent, fears about the death of his own children. Additionally, the very affection for children that motivated him to become a pediatrician makes it particularly painful for him to watch a child die.

As a result, the pediatrician often perceives the demands of the dying child and his family as overwhelming. He does not know how to mitigate their grief and he has already done everything that he knows how to do to save the child. He may be angry about his own helplessness and this anger is sometimes directed toward the child and his family who he feels are expecting more of him than should be expected of any human being. The author once knew a very capable, conscientious pediatric resident who had a ward patient who was dying as a result of cyclical vomiting. He had literally worked day and night to keep the child alive and heroic measures, including two sessions of non-contributory exploratory surgery, had been em-

---

* Research Associate, Research Foundation of Children's Hospital, Washington, D.C.

ployed. Yet for no reason which he could ascertain, the child continued to vomit and her condition was rapidly deteriorating. Finally, exhausted and enraged, he said to a supervisor, "I get so mad at that kid, sometimes I could slap her across the face. How dare she die in spite of everything I've done!"

Parents too feel impotent and helpless watching their child die, and the rage that results may be directed at the pediatrician either as an individual practitioner ("Why didn't you diagnose this sooner?") or as a representative of the medical profession ("Why haven't you doctors done something about this? If we can send a man to the moon, surely we can find a cure for leukemia!"). In addition to the parents' real anger, the pediatrician, sensitive about his inability to save the child, may perceive almost any of the parents' anguished questions ("Why did this have to happen?") as an attack upon him.

Occasionally the pediatrician will lose a patient for reasons which he might well consider the fault of the parents—the child who dies from a disease for which a vaccine is readily available; the baby who succumbs to head injuries incurred in a fall which could and should have been prevented; the child who could have been saved had his parents brought him to the doctor immediately after he was injured or when he first became ill. The pediatrician may feel furious not only because a child died needlessly, but because a patient of *his* died needlessly. His own anger may make it virtually impossible for him to do anything more than increase the parents' guilt.

As a result of all these factors, pediatricians, as well as other hospital personnel, frequently turn away from the dying child and his parents. The mother's phone calls are not returned or are returned only after considerable delay. Statements about the child's condition are relayed to the parents by a resident or a floor nurse. Visits to the child's bedside are made at times when the parents are likely to be absent. If the mother is seen coming down the hall, the doctor suddenly remembers something he must do elsewhere and leaves before she has seen him. Conversations with parents are brief and curt and confined to statements about the child's immediate condition.

When the moment of death comes, the pediatrician may be extremely brusque, even brutal about telling the parents. Having told them, he may simply leave the room. If he remains when they have begun to weep, he may say, "Don't cry. I did everything I could and you did, too", as if their weeping indicated regret about the care given the child. Unfortunately, it is often the pediatrician who cares most deeply about the child's death who is least able to break the news to the parents.

What can be done to help the pediatrician do a better job in what is admittedly an extremely painful situation? Primarily he needs to be helped long before he becomes a pediatrician, preferably from the first day of medical school. He needs to be taught to look at all patients not just at the molecular level or merely as conglomerates of inter-related physiological systems, but rather as total human beings who emotionally as well as physiologically are complex. He needs to appreciate that, for better or worse, most patients are part of a family, a family which cares deeply about them (although there are many tragic exceptions) and which strongly influences their physical and emotional health. Especially, he needs to appreciate the special problems of the dying patient and his family.

Training in dealing with the dying patient should come not only from experienced physicians but from mental health professionals, such as psychiatrists, psychologists and social workers. It should be a part of the curriculum at every medical school, and hospitals should sponsor regular symposia on the subject both for their residents and attending physicians. Material presented should be well thought out and offer specific guidance. Non-directive advice simply to "accept the patient's feelings" or overly generalized advice such as "never (or always) tell a patient he is dying", is not only useless but in some situations can be dangerous.

Someone once said, "we are all scared to death of dying," and the physician is no exception. Yet if he is truly to meet his obligation to his patients, he must come to grips with his own fear in order to help them with theirs.

Children's Hospital
Washington, D.C.

This article was reprinted from the *Archives of the Foundation of Thanatology*, Vol. II, No. 2, Copyright © 1970 by the Foundation of Thanatology.

Tears and Protest — A Mother's Remembrances

By Dalia Keyser*

"I have a terrible headache. It's the worst I've ever had." Kenny had come into the kitchen for aspirins and a glass of water. Without looking up from the task I was involved in I suggested the old standbys, the kind that helped minor ills through the years of raising a family. Kenny retreated to his room and the complaint was temporarily dismissed from my mind. There was only the fleeting thought that he might be coming down with a virus.

Later I wondered if he had come into the kitchen for reasssurance as well as aspirins. Did he already feel alarm over the strangely harsh sign that all was not well with him?

One month later, my husband Dorian and I learned the cruellest diagnosis. Fatal illness struck without warning. It singled out the child over whom I had been worrying the least—the oldest, the strongest, the best adjusted and seemingly most able.

This was the beginning of six months of suffering imposed by disease. Though it was the start of struggle it was as finalizing as the last day. That early summer date only marked complete dissolution of the crumpled shell that remained. It bore little resemblance to the husky boy of a half year earlier. In December everything was already decided for Kenny. The months that followed only carried out the havoc that caught us all off guard. Nothing in life could have prepared us. The odds were so small for Kenny to contact leukemia. Only one out of 20,000 is marked for it. Only one out of 7,000 children is hit by *any* form of cancer.

Illness came to Kenny while he still enjoyed the new pleasure of well-earned privileges. He was grateful for the independence and freedom he had at 16. His dependability and conscientiousness reaped the trust we had in his judgment. Driving was one measure of maturity he especially valued. Holding a part-time job and participating in organizational activity were other new additions. Primarily, however, Kenny had oriented himself this

---

* This article was excerpted from a book length manuscript by Mrs. Keyser.

fall towards good achievement in school. He had done outstandingly well last spring.

What place did illness have in the life of a gifted ambitious 16 year old boy? Where did it fit in? Kenny had taken his sound health for granted as everyone does when things go well. He appeared hardy and masculine with his solid frame—almost indestructable. But the disease quickly and treacherously gained an angry foothold, forcing Kenny's body to come into the foreground. He resisted and denied to himself those first weeks. Did he hope the disturbing effects would disappear if he refused to give in? Symptoms persisted, clamoring for attention and finally leaving him prostrate. In a way this initial period may have required the most drastic adjustment of Kenny. Bit by bit he was forced to recognize (not accept) the unpalatable fact of sickness. He had to relinquish the concept of himself as tough and beyond reach of physical infirmity. The disease had him against the wall. Once there was this first admission the rest was only a matter of stages. But all the way through Kenny seemed resolved to "take it" with dignity. And we decided to withhold the real gravity of the situation from him.

As I recall this period, I can't understand our dogged determination to plow through the Christmas holiday in the usual way. The tone was exaggerated, almost as though we knew our world would collapse soon afterwards. This was a frenzied attempt for normalcy, a last whistling in the dark before giving in to the disease dictator. But in the middle of recrimination I have wondered if Kenny wasn't helped by the busyness, disorder and good smells that permeated the kitchen. While he experienced bewildering physical discomfort could there have been reassurance in seeing the external setting as it always was during this season?

Kenny's appetite waned each day. He lost weight accordingly. It seemed to show most in his face which was drawn, though his clothes hung on him and he continually pulled his jeans up because his waist had dwindled so. At the last minute on Christmas Eve I began assembling ingredients for a tuna salad—there had been no time for more elaborate preparations. Kenny said at the table, "I'm sorry. I'm just not hungry." It was hard not to choke on my own food. I knew I should have allowed time to prepare something which would have been more tempting for him. The phrase was uttered often now and it haunted me, especially at night when I couldn't sleep. The image of his thin face haunted too. I began to feel deep fear.

One particular accident occurring before Christmas, affected me strangely. I was arranging greens lopsidely in a brandy snifter. I thought they were balanced finally and placed the container on the mantle. A few minutes later the sound of shattering glass told me I had been unsuccessful. Annoyed with myself I cleaned up the brick hearth with noisy disgruntlement. Kenny heard me and called out, "At least you can get another one." Reference was to the snifter. But somehow his words reverberated oddly—I heard them again and again during the months that followed. He was already telling me the lesson of my lifetime, that tears and protest should be reserved for irrevocable loss.

        ✿   ✿   ✿

[After 6 months of fruitless treatment, Kenny entered the hospital for the last time.] Whether to bolster himself, or me, or both, Kenny made it sound as though he had not yet given up, despite the crushing impact of return to the hospital. He said, "I hope I can get this thing licked once and for all. I don't want to miss any more school in the fall." I felt humble as I listened. He continued, "This really isn't too bad. Danny is my most galavanting friend and since he's going to work the first two weeks of vacation and travel with his family the third; he wouldn't be able to do anything with me now anyhow." I discerned the strain to be cheerful. Still he was determined to try rather than grovel in despair.

I told Kenny that Mrs. K. had donated blood in his name the previous afternoon. He responded, "I just don't know what to say. Everyone has done so much." How could I convince him that it was unnecessary and wrong to feel the weight of indebtedness? I reasoned—this is the way concerned people respond to trouble. I reminded him how we always reacted to others in distress. The shoe was simply on the other foot now and it was his turn to receive. He said, "This is some turn."

Earlier that same day I stood near his doorway when a hospital aide remarked over Kenny's substantial frame. She asked his age. I was shocked to hear myself answering, "He *would have* been 17 in August." How could I verbalize what I still didn't really believe.

Finally, the doctor told us, "The handwriting is on the wall." I pressed for something definite timewise but Dr. B. said it was too unpredictable—Kenny might hang on for days or only hours.

I asked about staying with Kenny around the clock. Doctor B. responded, "I sure would if it was my boy." But he cautioned that Kenny shouldn't feel the burden of our presence, the need to talk or keep up a front. He thought if we read a book (or even just pretended to) Kenny would have the comfort of our physical nearness without oppressiveness. I had a wild fear of Kenny meeting death without Dorian or me by his side.

Kenny's complaints were openly bitter now. Of the mouth dryness he said, "They tell me to try this and try that but nothing works." There was hopelessness. Then he added as though he felt the need to explain, "Maybe I'm just tired of being in the hospital." It felt to me like he was appealing for help. A parent is supposed to protect and comfort. Yet I continued to be powerless to change anything for him.

Though we decided against remaining with Kenny through the night (he seemed too alert and we feared the unusual might alarm him more) I was determined to stay till he was ready to sleep for the night. I went out to explain to the head nurse. She asked if Kenny feared the hospital. I told her his fright was related to his own imminent death. She wondered if frankness would help both him and me. Surely she was right but the advice was unthinkable for me now. I walked the precarious tightrope to keep functioning somehow—if I fell there would be total collapse and not even this superficial kind of support to offer Kenny.

That night when Dorian and I were going to sleep, he raised the question of donating Kenny's body for research. What if it would help shed some light on the mysterious disease? But the thought was impossible for either one of us. The suffering Kenny had endured in life was enough—he should at least be left in peace afterwards. I still cringed at open reference to "afterwards." But not as much as I had a month ago.

Dorian called around 8 A.M. to inquire how things were going. He said he would come as soon as our daughter Christine finished preparing her special Father's Day breakfast. Nadya later told me how difficult it was to stand by—Dorian was impatient to be off and Christine was engrossed in her painstaking preparations. She wanted things to be perfect for the occasion. She wouldn't accept help either. The breakfast project was the final test of Dorian's patience; he couldn't risk hurting Chris' feelings, especially on this day.

Dorian finally arrived at the hospital at mid-morning. The plan had been for him to stay now and for me to return to tell the girls what would be fact in a short time. Instead I panicked, Kenny might be gone by the time I returned. I went out and asked the nurse point blank how much longer she thought Kenny would last. She confessed she didn't see how it could be much longer. And so I refused to leave the hospital, burdening Dorian with the difficult and sad job of telling our two older daughters their brother would soon be gone. At this time I couldn't consider that Dorian too preferred to remain at the hospital in case Kenny expired in the interim. This wasn't the only instance when grief blinded and made my actions quite selfish.

After Dorian left Kenny approached delirium. He raved frantically about what he thought he saw and heard. He asked who the people on the ceiling were. One time he chanted, "I warned you, you're going to get in trouble." In desperation I tried to comfort him with physical closeness. I recognized how far gone he was when he didn't resist my holding him to me, in fact he seemed unaware. When Kenny lapsed into profound unconsciousness, the nurse asked if I felt more alone with the door shut? I realized I did so when she opened it for me. Then she drew the curtain around the foot of Kenny's bed so the hallway bustle wouldn't disturb him, though he appeared beyond disturbing now. Her sensitivity moved me. Later she returned, placed her hand on my shoulder and asked if I wanted her to sit with Kenny for a while. It was impossible for me to consider leaving his room, even for a minute. I could only shake my head. But her thoughtfulness was a priceless gift at that time. I felt less isolated after she left.

Meanwhile Kenny appeared disoriented. It was hard to watch more. I pleaded with the head nurse to contact our doctor for something more potent. Then the blow fell! I learned that he was not on call till noon, though his associate could be consulted. I felt unreasonably forsaken. Realistically it was irrelevant who did the prescribing now. But somehow things seemed worse knowing that the warm kindly Doctor who had tended Kenny since January was unreachable now. A young resident Doctor came in to confirm Kenny's condition. As she left Kenny chanted after her wildly, "You better hurry up, you better hurry up." The thought that he might realize how his time was running out almost paralyzed me for a moment. Dorian said afterwards he thought Kenny's directing might have had some relation to his backlog of anxiety about himself. Only last week at Cedars he had said to Dorian, "They better hurry and find a way to help my body make red blood cells."

Kenny and I were alone again. Only resounding inhalation within the oxygen mask broke the quiet. Nosebleeding and coughing finally subsided—the storm was ebbing toward a permanent still. Release started to come from deep within me. Kenny's unconscious state seemed to be the signal—it was at last safe to cry in his presence. But still there was impulse to check the tears. What if, by some miracle, Kenny would open his eyes to see open expression of grief, the thing I guarded against so fiercely for his sake? My arms ached to cradle his head but I felt driven to respect the way he preferred when he had all his faculties. Instead I put my arm next to his so that I could absorb his warmth while it still remained. The lunch tray was deposited on time without regard to what was happening in this particular hospital room. It appeared outrageously out of place, a harsh reminder that life goes on anyway!

Kenny's breathing became more uneven. The time between breaths was greatly drawn out. I tried to match my respiration to his but found I couldn't hold that long between inhaling and exhaling. Dorian had returned and we sat together, staring in disbelief. The pauses between breaths had grown so long that we began to expect the last one. My thumb was on the buzzer. I knew we wouldn't turn off the oxygen until we were sure. But the final breath was unmistakable when it came. It was accompanied by a very long groan. Then he was still. There was nothing to verify but the nurse rushed in in response to my automatic pressure on the buzzer. The head nurse tried to find a pulse. She couldn't be sure she wasn't feeling the vibrations in her own fingertips so she left for a stethoscope. Before she returned our doctor rushed in. Kenny was pronounced dead.

The nurses left discreetly. I was oblivious of everyone except Kenny. Even Dorian was shut out. I kissed Kenny over and over again as I hadn't done when he was alive. I was aware of deep anger when I said, "You didn't have a chance."

Doctor B. offered gently,

"Would you like a sedative, Mrs. Keyser?"

I lashed back, "Who am I to need a sedative?" The idea of accepting a crutch for myself after all the suffering Kenny was subjected to was abhorrent to me. Finally I remembered Dorian. He was directly behind me. We found each other and cried together for the first time.

Peace had come to Kenny's face swiftly. Even his mouth, arrested in its struggle for breath and still bearing traces of the hemorrhaging, did not detract from an over-all impression of serenity. It was impossible not to feel relief for him. His overdose of pain and suffering was over.

The door opened a few times. Doctor B. attempted to draw the sheet over Kenny's face. I began to feel annoyed. I asked, "What's the rush?" Death had been in such a hurry to claim our boy. Why couldn't we be allotted uninterrupted time to digest the facts?

Dorian and I reiterated Kenny's fondness for our doctor and he spoke of the fineness he admired in Kenny. He thought the courage and inner strength Kenny exhibited were rare for a person of any age. We spoke of the disease and our concern that there must be a cure found, even though it would come too late for Kenny. He expressed bitterness over the begging that must be done in order to achieve funds for continued research.

The nurses sensitively packed Kenny's things while we were in the other room. They meant to spare us more pain. I kissed each one "good-bye." Their tears mingled with mine.

We left with Kenny's suitcase, concrete evidence of our bereavement.

Two and a half weeks after Kenny was gone I found myself starting this record in its crudest form. Instead of being comforted by relatives and friends who stayed close by I was impatient and annoyed. I needed to start assimilating the facts at a deeper level. It could only be done in the solitude which I craved desperately.

My original intent was the straightforward account of Kenny's illness. I thought I wanted it for the girls. They were shut out for six months—we couldn't risk sharing the truth with them for fear it would be transmitted inadvertently back to Kenny. In a vague way I must have been thinking this might compensate for the openess they were deprived of earlier. When I explained to Christine what I was doing she didn't seem surprised. She said, "I thought you would do something like that."

There was a compulsion to write while the facts were still fresh in mind. I felt like I was hanging on to them quite frantically, as though they might slip away from me as Kenny had. But once everything was said, there was a kind of emotional purgation.

The initial draft accomplished original aims but it left me feeling dissatisfied. I had only just begun to look; there needed to be a true scrutiny of feelings. This was the time to stand still and study. Running on would be no good—there was no place where guilt and regret would not follow. Also I wanted intuitively to extend the writing time because it kept me feeling closer to Kenny. In fact, the idea of being positively "through" brought real panic.

As internal turmoil was explored I felt more at ease. I wrote as I couldn't talk, and still can't, even to Dorian. He grappled with the hurt in his own way. He couldn't hear mine too, even though the source was one and the same. When I tried talking to others, I either broke down or my listeners decided it would be better for me to talk about something else. So it was that I was restricted to expressing guilt, hurt and anger on paper till I myself was overwhelmed at the endless flow. As I wrote, everything seemed very personal. Later I wondered, how unique could these feelings be? Aren't they really shared by every parent who has lost a child?

Eulogizing was unconscious. Probably it stemmed from the basic guilt we felt for having survived Kenny. There had been so little time to appreciate and we had taken for granted that there would be a lifetime ahead in which to enjoy him. Now there was too little to remember and too much time to remember it in.

Since there has been much pain in the fact that we never knew Kenny's innermost feelings about his illness there has been compulsion to dwell in this area of regret. The wonder of Kenny's choice to maintain a strong image no matter what received much attention too. I reviewed qualities which seemed to have added up to this—sensitivity to others, dignity, courage and above all the innate hope of youth, that jewel-like trust that the bad will be overcome somehow. Our decision to withhold truth imposed on him the game of pretend—pretend that death from the disease was not inevitable. This was always the real culprit. Would we ever become reconciled to the only way we had been able to function—now that there was limitless time to review the restrictive hurt of it? In time I found peace over one point. During the illness Kenny sometimes needed to deny to himself. Because the truth had not been inflicted there was leeway for this temporary escape. What if such small relief had been closed to him? And yet when he felt up to it he could face what he must have known in his heart to be true. While Kenny was alive and for a long time afterwards I couldn't tolerate the idea that he understood what was happening to him. I was angered when people intimated, carrying an unreasonable suspicion that they were pushing something on me which I was unready to face.

Once a friend asked if I thought the record, when completed, would be helpful to other troubled parents in a similar plight? My answer was unequivocally negative. We had no fool-proof formulas to pass on. We had not weathered so well that we could advise others. Our predicament was not singular but the combination of our personalities was. I remember well during Kenny's illness how it upset me to hear the fate of other leukemic children. Because I was so unprepared to relinquish him I used to argue with myself, "It won't happen to us that way. Kenny's case will turn out differently." Reading of the sad experience of others would be just as detrimental during the time of trauma. During the period of rehabilitation, however, bereft parents might feel less alone when they learn that others have experienced thoughts and feelings so much like their own. The conviction that no one quite understands, chief contributor to the illusion of isolation with personal misery, would begin to weaken. Warmth and comfort come from sharing anything, even grief.

Brushing by these pages several years later I am startled. Was all this mine? The pain stands out so raw and naked. The years that have elapsed have also made it possible for me to look now at the wrongness of keeping truth from Kenny and to see what I couldn't bear to see before. Nature protected me from deeper understanding before I was ready for it. And I shudder over that terrible decision even while I am unsure we could do differently if faced with the same dilemma again. One thing remains unchanged as time goes on, the desire to "do" something about the disease that took Kenny's life. It is not possible to remain with quiet acceptance while such a killer is still on the loose. The search for a niche where I can contribute still goes on.

The Widow's View of Her Dependent Children[1]

By Phyllis Silverman, Ph.D.* and Sue Englander, M.S.S.**

With the growing awareness of the problems a woman must face when she becomes widowed, the needs of others who are dependent upon her, her children, come into focus as well. Widowhood is usually thought to be a problem of the older years when children are already grown. As we look at total populations of widows, we find that this is not true. A woman widowed in her fifties, with a large family, could have several young children at home, and since more and more women are marrying late or postponing their childbearing years until they are over 30, many more will find themselves raising young children alone. A study in 1962 shows 627,000 widow-child families in the United States with 2.2 million paternal orphans in these families under the age of 18. We can presume that these numbers grow and a recent estimate reported that one out of every five children in the United States will be orphaned, that is, one parent will die before he reaches the age of 16.

It is the purpose of this paper to report on some of the experiences of such young people when they become paternal orphans at the time their mother is widowed. The children discussed here were those whose mothers were served by the Widow-to-Widow Program. This program was an experiment in preventive intervention in which every newly-widowed woman under the age of 60, in a lower middle-class community of 250,000 was contacted by another widow for the purpose of providing her with friendship and help during this critical period after the death of her husband. Four hundred and thirty women were reached in a

---

[1] Prepared for Presentation at the Symposium on Dying and Bereavement, Berkeley, California, March, 1973. Sponsored by NIMH. This article is published in *OMEGA*, Vol. 6, #1, 1975. Reprinted here with their permission.

* Dr. Silverman is a lecturer on Social Welfare in the Department of Psychiatry, Harvard Medical School, Laboratory of Community Psychiatry, 58 Fenwood Road, Boston, Massachusetts 02115.

** Ms. Englander is a Staff Social Worker, Greater Lawrence Mental Health Center, Lawrence, Massachusetts.

period of two and a half years. Two-thirds of these chose to involve themselves in the program, if not soon after the death, then within a year. Of those who accepted, fifty-two had children under the age of 16 at home, and of those who refused, twelve had children in this age group.

A review of the literature reveals a paucity of data about childhood bereavement.* However, the death of a parent during childhood is significantly correlated with adult problems. Most data only examine the adult populations in psychiatric treatment.

The few prospective studies of bereaved children are presented as case studies of individuals in treatment. There is consensus that the bereaved child has a higher than chance risk of developing serious problems as an adult. It has been found that individuals who lost a parent in childhood were more likely to commit suicide successfully than those who had not had such a loss.

Several studies have noted the high rate of parental loss experienced by delinquent populations. It has been suggested that boys and girls who dropped out of high school prematurely, in relation to a parental loss, may have done so as a consequence of the expectation that these students would assume wage-earning and homemaking roles of the deceased partner of the same sex. It could also be a result of the lack of an appropriate identification model and suitable parental controls. Kastenbaum (1959) also suggests that the adolescent may have particular difficulty incorporating the concept of death into his life plan because this is a period when he is striving for mastery of his own life. Death is something which brings out his sense of helplessness and ability to control his world.

Not all sequelae are pathological. The hypothesis has also been made that scientific genius is positively associated with parental loss to death in childhood. Though this hypothesis has not been sufficiently tested, one child in five is expected to lose a parent in the twentieth century, and amongst eminent scientists, two out of five have lost a parent. Parental bereavement must have some psychological effect on the child but it is necessary to learn more about the surrounding circumstances that lead to these various outcomes.

---

* The literature review has been presented in digested form here in deference to the more general nature of this publication. It appears in full form in Dr. Silverman's article in *Omega*.

In looking at the surrounding circumstances that affect how a child grieves, we are seeking to learn what does seem to make the difference in how he accommodates to his father's death. It becomes important to identify patterns of withdrawal, indications of the assumption of more responsibility than is appropriate for his age, the family's ability to accept each other's grief and to talk about what has happened, the mother's ability to maintain her maternal role, and to see in what way the child is able to maintain a sense of ability to master his world. It is not the presence or absence of any of these factors that will matter, but what patterning occurs. Our primary interest is in trying to prevent emotional disabilities from developing in these children. We are looking, then, for those patterns that may lead to the most difficulty and to see if we can determine what would be helpful to improve the situation.

The data for this paper were drawn from the follow-up interviews, three years after the mother became widowed, with the widow evaluating the effect of the Widow-to-Widow service or discussing her reasons for refusing. In addition there were limited process records kept of the intervention, where the widow talked about her children and what was happening now that their father was dead. The data have many limitations; among them is that the children were not the focus of the intervention nor the research and, therefore, were not interviewed for their views of what was happening. The view here is from the mother's side of the equation. Her children were another variable with which she had to cope as she struggled with her own grief. These are children under 16 who still need mothering and fathering to varying degrees and what happened to them would depend in large part on their parent's ability first to see their needs and then respond to them. The paper reports the widow's view of her child (children)'s reaction to the death of their father; problems she had with the children as a result; how she coped and what help was available and what help she did use in solving any problems she had with the children.

The youngest widow in this group was 23 when the husband died leaving her with two small children, the oldest was in her 50's and she had a 12-year old son at home. The majority of the women were white working-class Catholics reflecting the composition of the community served. There was one Jewish woman in the group reflecting the fact that this small segment of the community was primarily elderly. There were several black families, again reflecting their proportion in the population. Death came suddenly in most cases; however, some men had had extended illnesses which to some extent brought them closer to the children. Since they had been unable to work, they had spent more time at home with their children.

In three families we learned about the father's gambling, drinking and that the mother had threatened divorce or was separated. The fact that there were children under 16 at home was most consistently significant when we tried to determine what affected people's accepting or refusing the offer of help (Silverman 1971). It seemed that having dependent children at home made a bereaved woman acutely aware of her widowed status and, therefore, more responsive to an offer of help from another widow who could provide some real guidance in managing her new situation.

In trying to understand this complex data it is necessary to find some way of presenting it in an orderly fashion to the reader which takes it beyond the individual case and allows for some generalization from the material. We have taken a sample of the cases, 19. These are white Protestant and Catholic families with 56 children among them. Of these about fifteen are over sixteen. We tried to abstract the various reactions of mother and children on certain common dimensions. This is not a normative approach that is used in statistical analysis but one that examines trends, typical reactions and allows the reader to see some of the interactions that take place between them and to become involved in some of the complexities. We are not verifying hypotheses. Hopefully we will generate a few.

The Widow's View of Her Child's Reactions— *Accepting Each Other's Grief*

Most widows do not remember how they told their children that their father was dead. The period around the death event was a blur to many of them. No matter at what age the child reacted with a sense of disbelief or denial. One ten year old beat up his older sister who told him the news when he came home from school. A three year old asked when daddy was coming back. Most of these mothers felt that the children had done fine, they had cried and then seemed all right. The child's denial, disbelief, or sense of shock was taken to mean that the child did not understand or appreciate what had happened and therefore was not in mourning. However phrases like "they were crushed," "he became very quiet," "hard to know—he couldn't sleep nights," and "they were heartbroken" kept coming up in the conversation.

Almost all the older children, eight years and above went to the wake if not the funeral. Only one mother thought this helpful to her children in accepting the death. The others were primarily concerned that the funeral might upset the child more than necessary, that they would break down and cry. This was not sufficient reason to keep them home. One mother made an agreement with her adolescent son that they would not cry at the funeral and arranged a signal to remind each other if one weakened. Another mother, recalling her own fear as an adolescent at her mother's funeral, did not take her six year old because she thought it would be too frightening. The most vivid thing one mother remembered about her children at the funeral was that the oldest girl (eighteen) would not look into the coffin because she wanted to remember her father as he was. The point here is that this group could not express strong feelings easily and preferred to shy away from them since the members did not know how to cope with them easily. One mother was sorry she took her eleven year old to the first anniversary mass. He became so upset he couldn't stop crying. She saw no positive value in this expression of feelings.

Most women during the first year were struggling with their own acceptance of the new reality they now faced without a spouse. They found the children's questions about the death and its meaning most painful, "like sticking a knife in me." Several women found themselves avoiding discussions about their husbands so as not to have to answer questions. They also felt that the children would be unduly upset by seeing their own grief, and therefore, tried to keep from crying in front of the children. One woman said that it made her feel more lonely but that she "can't go around mourning in front of grown boys." In some few families, mother and children rarely grieved in front of each other so that even two years later when one of the boys (now nineteen) found his father's driving license he filled up with tears and left the room. Most people found that this did not work over a long period of time.

I tried to keep my feelings from them. A friend, a priest, told me not to and so did Dorothy (the aide) and in the end I let them see my sadness and crying. Now we each share our feelings more honestly. It has brought us closer together.

In another family, the two daughters did talk about their father until they saw how upset their mother became. In order to prevent her from crying they stopped asking. In contrast, their thirteen year old brother became very quiet, never even trying to mention his father.

Children can misunderstand their mother's silence and think that their mother does not miss their father or care about him. One woman whose children were eleven, ten, and eight said:

> *We've come a long way since then. I was shocked to discover that they thought I didn't care. This came out when I was talking to my eleven year old's teacher. I had to force myself to talk about their father, and to cry in front of them, and to help them keep their very good memories of him. I don't want them to ever forget their father, and I guess that's what they thought I wanted when I didn't show my feelings.*

In most families, mother and children found a way of talking about the deceased, often because someone outside the family pointed out the consequences of what they were doing. One mother said "we talk about him often but it is like he is on vacation." Ways seem to be found to temper the sense of loss. One young adolescent comforted his mother with the thought that his father is "with Jesus" trying to reassure her there is no reason for the extent of her sadness; and another girl now nine, who was six when her father died, prays to him every night, and constantly asks if he is watching her and if he would be proud of her.

To the statement that Daddy was in heaven with God, one three year old asked "if his father would have his fun clothes on when he stayed with God." One woman told her adolescent children "Your father will always be with us." In other families, the mother noticed that some of the children would go to the cemetery very regularly to visit the grave. One adolescent had given up religion but since his father's death goes to formal worship once a month on the day he died.

There was some bed wetting and sleeplessness in one or two younger children. This was transitory. One six year old who did become eneuretic, had a great need to talk about his father who was killed in an automobile accident. He played "crash" over and over again with his cars for several months.

These women were not aware that their children talked to others outside the home about their father. In the above case, this boy did talk at school. Fortunately he found a sympathetic and helpful teacher who, the mother learned, was encouraging him to talk with her about his loss.

These women were not prepared to connect their children's behavior with their feelings about their father dying. Children had different reactions, some more obvious than others. One fifteen year old, the youngest of three, was described by her mother:

> *Her room had been plastered with pictures of the Beatles. The day her father died she went up and took them down. She said "I'm not a baby any more Mom." I tried to explain to her that she was still a child, even if her father had died. But I guess when you go through something like that you never feel the same. The pictures never went back up.*

This child, in a sense, grew up overnight. However, she did not express her grief in any other way and this is a family which avoids talking about anything that they think would upset someone. To share would be to burden the individual. Mother explained that she is very independent and, therefore, does not share her feelings.

Mother's Ability to Maintain Her Maternal Role

All of these women felt that their children gave meaning to their lives at a time when they felt despair and hopelessness. For some this involved their remaining alert and involved to respond to their children's needs. For others this meant that they had someone to lean on, to get them up and out of themselves, implying that they may have been getting more than giving even from young children.

There seemed to be three reactions to the surviving parent that the widows observed in different children which related to their own behavior and involvement: the child became terrified that he would lose the surviving parent; the child assumed special responsibilities in the family in taking care of others; and the child who became rebellious, who withdrew socially and whose school work fell off. It was this latter group which caused their mothers the most concern, often with cause. One child out of many in a family had an extreme reaction. Most often these seemed to be boys between the ages of eleven and fourteen. In two other situations, teenage daughters were involved. There is not enough data to see how these several responses intertwined with each other in one child but we have no reason to believe that they are discrete entities. One example is available in a family where the oldest child is six. Mother is talking.

> *I was very tired. I don't know how I took care of the babies that year. I relied on my oldest to help. This had forced her to be mature and more self-reliant. If I needed to run out to the store for a minute I had to let her watch the babies. About ten months after my husband died she had a dream that I was lying on the couch making noises. She got pills which did not help. I tried to reassure her that I wasn't going anywhere.*

This is the same mother noted earlier, who about this time began to consciously share her grief with her children. However, we can assume that they sensed her incapacity all along.

We are not talking about neglect; we are talking about preoccupation. There were two mothers in this overall group of fifty-two families who did neglect their children leaving them with baby sitters and older siblings. This, however, was their typical way of managing. One of these women had abandoned the children to her husband for six months before he died. Upon his death these children were indeed orphaned and lost both parents; in the other family, father and mother had been separated for three months before he died and nothing changed for the children when this happened as far as the attention they got from their mother.

The fear of losing the surviving parent is very real. One woman said that her youngest, age eight, had nightmares shortly after her father died which she wasn't sure were connected to his death:

> *She had a dream about me being taken away from her, or she couldn't find her way home—or it always seemed as if she found herself alone at the end of the dream or nightmare.*

As she talked she then realized that her middle daughter, age ten, wouldn't let her mother leave the house unless she knew where she was going, who was driving, and when she would be home.

> *If I came home five minutes late she was a nervous wreck. I guess that's how it affected them, not in the usual way in tears and crying and the grief you naturally expect.*

Without interpreting or understanding the behavior as a reaction to the death, she had responded by being there when they needed her. It is important to keep in mind this mother's comment that she typically expected the grief to be expressed directly in tears and sadness. Because most women had similar thoughts they didn't connect other unusual behavior with grieving. Until they could see the link here, some women indulged their children reluctantly because they feared spoiling them or worried, now that father was gone, that they did not want to let the children think they could get away with things.

One twelve year old boy whose father had been murdered in his front hall refused to go back and forth to school unless escorted by his mother. She recognized his real fear of the neighborhood but also that his clinging was a result of his fear of losing her. It took her awhile to realize that having these problems was "no sin."

A six year old only child expressed her fear of losing her mother by insisting that she walk her home from school every day. One woman pointed out that her children were paralyzed by seeing her cry on the anniversary of their father's death. It may be that children's inability to let mother cry in front of them is a result of their understanding that they lose her as well to her grief. A younger child who is perhaps more ingenuous, less fearful of saying what he thinks, asked directly: "Who will take care of me if something happens to you?"

The assumption of additional responsibility is a more subtle phenomenon to assess and describe. It can be seen in a twelve year old girl's admonition to her mother: "Don't cry while we are at school." This mother talked more about all three girls:

> They didn't want to go to school at first. They worried about me at home alone. When I insisted they go I think they were glad to get out of the house. They also said that my middle girl who is closest to me would always stay by me so I didn't have to be alone when they grew up.

Another woman whose children are older adolescents (again it is the girls in the family) talked about how they worry over her:

> They try to get me out, over my depression. I'd be lost without them. They protect and baby me from all the sadness I feel. I almost had a breakdown after my husband died.

Working helped me, too. Everyone there worked, at keeping me busy and occupied.

This is a family where the children take care of the parents. This mother did it for her own mother who was widowed at age thirty-three and now her daughters are doing it for her. For this, this mother is very grateful.

One woman said her older girls "became women, they were very brave and very helpful." She though it must be very hard for a woman with no older children. Another woman who had made the agreement not to cry at the funeral saw this son:

. . . as a charm. He's never been anything but courage and encouragement to me. If he cried, which he did with his older brother and sister, he never let me see it.

None of the behavior described to date gave the parents much trouble. They seemed able to reassure their children that they would take care of them. The children did not seem to be over-whelmed by what they gave their mother in part because these were reciprocal relationships. The widowed mother seemed able to continue mothering these girls and to consider their needs. We assume this from the fact that most of these girls have done well, have gone on to finish school and some have gone away to college.

These women were at a loss to understand or to know how to respond to those children who withdrew, began doing poorly in school, and seemed to lose purpose and direction. These were primarily boys, and usually from nine to fourteen years of age. This group of five children from five families included one adolescent girl who withdrew completely from school initially and then from all activities outside of the house. About her brothers the mother said:

They had a rough time. One was his father's alter-ego. They had a sense of responsibility and kept going. My daughter just stopped living.

These were all youngest or middle children with older sisters. All these children enjoyed a special relationship to their father. One went so far as to tell his mother, "Why couldn't it have been you instead of Daddy." The girl did tell her mother, "I am closer to Daddy than you are." She spent a good deal of time caring for her father (after school and on weekends) during his terminal illness when he was at home and mother worked. In another situation in which the withdrawal occurred immediately after the death and was a transitory symptom, this mother saw her boy's problem:

> *He's the only man in the house. He must feel picked on. His father used to protect him from me. I was the firm disciplinarian.*

Several of these women talked about the boys' need for discipline; a boy needs a father. "If his father was alive he would have made him work, he was more scared of his father." They saw the role of father to some extent involving a police function, but more than that it was in getting the boys to perform properly. In studying the patterns in what happens to these children, it seems to be that the problem is less in terms of the children's need for control but more in terms of how they saw their role in the family vis-à-vis the mother. These women had a special relationship to their other children, usually girls of the sort described above, and they closed out the boys. The boy, in a sense, did lose both parents. He seemed unable to get close to his mother and looked to his father to help him break away from the dependency relationship with his mother, to show him how to link himself to the outside world, to be a separate individual. At his father's death he felt helpless to know how to complete these tasks. His solution was to withdraw and thereby now to try to involve mother in a more extensive care-giving role than she would normally have had or would be appropriate for his age.

Some of these women talked about these boys as wanting to assume the role of a father.* One, as the only son, had been told directly by relatives, that this was expected of him. Another boy had been his father's favorite; now his mother says that he knows he is just like the rest. He talked about assuming his father's place which involved giving orders and being waited on by the woman in the family. He gave this up when he realized that his mother would not allow him to behave this way. The problem disappeared when the widowed mother realized what was happening and made it clear that the boys were not to assume this

---

* This can be seen as one way of keeping father around if one succeeds in being like him.

responsibility—it was inappropriate to their age and role in the family.

The problem seemed to continue when the mother had no idea what was going on, was getting a good deal from the other children and, in fact, was encouraging her son to be like his father. The child who was giving her trouble didn't seem able to do this successfully. As one woman put it:

> *My oldest boy takes on more responsibility. He has absorbed his father's goodness. He is always asking me if I am all right and if I am happy.*

This is the same mutuality she enjoys with her daughters while her youngest son keeps talking about his father:

> *He idealizes him. He still talks about the way his father punished him as better than the ways his friends' fathers treat their children now. He really worries me. I think some of his answering back is adolescence, but he is becoming a loner, he won't go to Scouts anymore, he's withdrawn and talks about wanting to be an artist.*

This woman allows her boy to get some fathering from a male relative but belittles his ability since he does not have her husband's intellectual scope. She is concerned about this boy's withdrawal. Another woman who sees herself protected by her children from her grief talks about her youngest child and only son who, like his mother, never talks about his feelings:

> *He is very emotional. He drives and every once in awhile he goes to visit his father's grave. He talks a lot about his father. I keep saying to him, "you'd better grow up and be like your father" and he says "I will Ma."*

She went on:

> *He's not like his father though. My husband was so quiet, but in sports they were alike. But his grades have gone down. He's stopped paying attention. He seems to live in a world of his own.*

With one exception, these were all men who were very much involved with their families. Some were considered gentle leaving discipline and the like to their wives, others were the disciplinarians and pace-setters for the family. Their relationship to their wives seemed to be good as well. The exception was a man who was a compulsive gambler whose wife had threatened divorce. His older daughter was relieved by his death since he had a repressive attitude toward women, and his son tried to develop a similar privileged position, but mother would not allow this to happen, as noted above. This child did not withdraw.

The data do not permit further elaboration of this pattern at this point. (To say more, we need to read all 64 cases and to talk with the children.) The withdrawal and becoming ineffectual seems to be related to the child's position in the family, usually the only surviving male, and to the way his mother does her mothering, at least when she is bereaved. At this point she sees the children as giving her purpose and meaning, and helping her to keep going, and is not sensitive to any special taking care of that they may need now that their father is gone. The child we are focusing on now seems to have had unfinished business with his father, which was helping him move away from mother, and learning how to function independently outside the home (S.M. Silverman, 1974). The child's behavior indicates a sense of helplessness, a sense of ineffectuality in the face of the conflict he is experiencing, and so he gives up. His mother's behavior does seem to make a difference in what happens in the long run. As she becomes aware and is able to respond to his special needs he seems to do better.

Helping Resources

A mother's use of help depends in part on how she defines her problems and how she understands her own ability to change things. It is also dependent upon the accidents of fate that placed, for example a child in a classroom with a sensitive teacher. All these women accepting of the offer of assistance from the widow aide, felt that they had something to learn from her. Even in this they were different.

Most of them defined the help offered by the aide in terms of their needs. Several women found that they simply needed to ventilate their feelings and once this was done they were able to go on and solve their own problems themselves. For example, one woman whose children were all in the teens talked about her late night phone calls to the aide:

> *I used to feel as if I was going to burst. After I talked to Mary I would feel better. I had a lot of problems. It isn't*

clear if it would have happened if my husband had lived. He was stricter. My daughter in college got pregnant. Everyone was talking abortion. I knew it wouldn't be good for her. I tried to let her decide by giving her support, telling her what choices she had. We kept the baby and now welfare will pay for her to finish college. She was an honor student.

In this family, one daughter married and mother thinks it was because she was embarrassed by her younger sister keeping her baby. This was her way of getting out of the house. She seems to be doing well as did the rest of the family members who seemed able to utilize resources around them well. Mother used the insurance money she received to move out of the old neighborhood where the schools were bad and it was becoming dangerous to go out at night. She bought a house in a nice suburban community. All the children are achieving at school, have been offered college scholarships, and so forth.

Women with small children seemed to ask for more guidance in how to manage, and did focus on the problems they had with the children. They had a great need to talk, and found this satisfied only when talking to another widow who had faced similar problems of the special loneliness that comes from trying to care for little children alone. They worried about what was best for their children, but most unbearable for them were the long evening hours after the children were in bed, and the house became empty. One mother, age 23, who remarried a year later was most fearful that her two year old's paternal grandparents would turn him against his step-father by constantly reminding him who his "real" father was. She had decided that she would not allow him to visit alone if this kept up and sought support in the correctness of this idea. However, she primarily needed to share her isolation and despair. This need lasted for about six months.

Those children who developed a withdrawn life style came from homes where the attitudes about help were very similar. Only one mother in this group was ultimately pushed by her daughter's behavior to seek professional psychiatric guidance. None of these women talked easily about their feelings and found it most difficult to allow the aide into their lives. They got a good deal of specific assistance from friends and family, but to get involved in a new friendship seemed too frightening and made them fearful that they would thereby lose their independence. Reactions ranged from reluctance from an awareness and special acceptance of their interdependency with others, to a denial of any need for such intimacy and refusal to ever really talk about themselves. These are not seriously damaged people from a psychological point of view. They enjoyed the aide, they got something from knowing another widow; from expanding their social horizons to make new friends in a group setting; they got encouragement to go back to work. They rarely talked about the children as problems.

Some women needed someone else to point out their children's difficulty. However, it did not always lead to any action. Most of them normalized the difficulty by attributing part of it to adolescence (which cannot be discounted). Several mothers did nothing but worry. One mother, never really in charge of the situation as she saw herself, found her boy failed by several teachers in a private school who never talked to her or her son about the difficulties he began to have. She seemed quietly overwhelmed by the whole thing, and finally at someone else's suggestion put him in another school, never really talking over with her son what could be causing his current problems. She never responded to the aide's encouragement to initiate some conversation with her son about his father.

In this sample of nineteen only two women sought help from a formal mental health agency. In one such case it took the mother more than two years to do anything. The second situation involved a child whose father had been murdered and who had been inappropriately placed in classes for the retarded many years before. This woman would always be involved in agencies. She managed money poorly, and was often close to financial disaster. She seemed at times more interested in complaining than learning to budget better. With the aide's encouragement the mother began to seek help for her son to place him in another school and to determine what part of his difficulty was caused by his father's death, and what part by his early disability that led to the classification of retarded. First with the aide, and finally three years later with a child guidance clinic, this mother is changing and the boy has been placed in regular graded classes and is doing well.

In four situations mothers found the school helpful. This was not because they recognized that their child might have difficulty or that the school should even be informed about the father's death. Most often the teacher learned from the child what had happened, and then observing changes in him tried to be supportive and listen to the child. In one instance the teacher called when an eleven year old told her about his being the man in the family now. She linked his behavior to the death and the way the family was reacting. She called the mother as did another teacher who noticed a first grader's unusual quietness and sadness. These mothers appreciated the teachers' help and learned something about their children from it.

On the whole, these mothers felt that their other relatives offered them little sustained assistance during the first year of bereavement with the specific problems related to their widowhood. One woman likened her relatives' involvement to "traffic slowing down to go past an accident and then speeding up again." The frequent offers of help from family during the first few months rapidly dwindle during the course of the first year until the widows find themselves very much alone. The widows felt that their grief was a burden to friends and relatives who expected them to resume life as usual. Nonetheless, there was a good deal of interaction with their families and much of their social lives revolved around this.

The widow-aide was described by all the women as someone with whom they did not have to feign strength, but in whom they could confide feelings of hopelessness and despair. Since the aide had experienced a loss, she could truthfully assure the widows that their grief was normal. The widows report that they were then better able to recognize their grief as time-limited. Local family doctors intervened with three families to help anticipate the death and to prescribe anti-depressants. In one family, a local priest provided a young widow with a supportive relationship.

Discussion and Implication

It is essential to understand why these widows often did not focus explicitly on their children's behavior as a response to loss when the range of behavior they described demonstrates that their children did react. For however brief a time period, these children conveyed their feelings in their own language, often in concrete behavior change regardless of their age. This was evident even as their mothers depicted them as unaffected.

We can account for this in several ways. 1) In a society where the ritualistic supports to the newly bereaved have broken down, the widows' responses to their children in part reflect the culture's evasion and confusion. This is reflected in the widow's dismay and surprise that her child or children did not show the same degree of depression she was feeling.

2) The second reason the widow cannot focus on her child's needs comes from her own grief. She clearly communicates to him: "Don't show me you're upset." By insulating the child from her own grief, the widow protects herself. Avoidance and denial are employed to protect themselves and their children from the painfulness of the loss. James Agee's novel *A Death in the Family* vividly captures how the child senses his parent's unwillingness to discuss the death:

> *When you want to know more—about it (and her eyes become still more vibrant) just ask me, just, just ask me and I'll tell you because you ought to know. "How did he get hurt" Rufus wanted to ask, but he knew by her eyes that she did not mean at all what she said, not now anyway, not this minute, he need not ask; and now he did not want to ask because he too was afraid; he nodded to let her know he understood her.* (Agee, 1957, p. 253)

3) A third reason for the widow not responding related to the extent to which she was normally attuned to her children's needs and modes of communication before the death. Only a relatively small number in this community made it part of their role as mother to understand their children's concerns and to look behind the behavior, or to worry about what being a good mother means. In a recent unpublished study of La Leche League for nursing mothers (Silverman and Murrow, 1973) it was noted that members of this group from the community in which all the Widow-to-Widow program was conducted, do not display any guilt about their ability to be good mothers. They learned their role from their own mothers and have no conflict about what being a good mother means or how to behave in this role. Therefore, we can presume in their widowhood they would not change their style.

This involves us in a comparative analysis of working-class styles of mothering or parenting with those that are more middle class. We need to learn more about grieving in other communities to see if the vacuum exists in knowing how to respond and therefore the pre-occupation with the meaning of behavior and extra-ordinary desire to be sensitive to children's needs may break down. This is not to imply that the family is not in tune to the child's developmental needs. Rather they are understood and responded to in different ways and these ways are further disrupted by the grief.

4) Finally, it is essential to discuss the deviant child, the one who withdraws and who in some ways is grieving more traditionally since he becomes quiet, and in many ways may be depressed.

BIBLIOGRAPHY

Birtchnell, J., "Depression in Relation to Early and Recent Parent Death," *British Journal of Psychiatry*, 116, 1970, pp. 299-306.

Bonnard, A., "Truancy and Pilfering Associated With Bereavement" in *Adolescents: Psychoanalytic Approach to Problems and Therapy*, Loand and Schneer (Eds.), New York, Harper Bros., 1961, pp. 152-79.

Bowlby, J., "Grief and Mourning in Infancy and Childhood" *The Psychoanalytic Study of the Child*, New York: International Univ. Press, 1960, pp. 9-52.

Brown, F., "Childhood Bereavement and Subsequent Psychiatric Disorder," *British Journal of Psychiatry*, Vol. 112, 1966, pp. 1035-1042.

Cain, A.C., I. Fast, and M. Erickson, "Children's Disturbed Reactions to the Death of a Sibling," *American J. of Orthopsychiatry*, Vol. 34, 1964, pp. 741-752.

Dorpat, T. L., and J. K. Jackson, and H. S. Ripley, "Broken Homes and Attempted and Completed Suicide," *Archives of General Psychiatry*, Vol. 12, 1965, pp. 213-216.

Glick, Paul C., "The Life Cycle of the Family," *Marriage and Family Living*, Vol. 17, 1955, pp. 3-9.

Greer, S., "Study in Parental Loss in Neurotics and Sociopaths," *Archives of General Psychiatry*, Vol. 11, 1964, pp. 177-80.

Gregory, Ian, "Anteretrospective Data Following Childhood Loss of a Parent," *Archives of General Psychiatry*, Vol. 13, 1965, pp. 110-20.

Kastenbaum, R., "Time and Death in Adolescents," in *The Meaning of Death*, H. Feifel (Ed.), New York, McGraw-Hill, 1965, pp. 99-113.

Markusen, E. and R. Fulton, "Childhood Bereavement and Behavior Disorders, A Critical Review," *Omega*, Vol. 2, 1971, pp. 102-117.

Munroe, A., "Childhood Loss in a Psychiatrically Normal Population," *British Journal of Psychiatry*, Vol. 19, 1965, pp. 69-79.

Newman G. and S. Denman, "Felony and Paternal Deprivation A Socio-Psychiatric View," *International J. of Social Psychiatry*, Vol. XVIII, No. 1, 1971, pp. 65-71.

Silverman, S. M., "Parental Loss in Scientists," *Science Studies*, July, 1974, Vol. 4, pp. 259-264.

Silverman, P. R., "Factors Involved in Accepting an Offer of Help," *Archives of Foundation of Thanatology*, Vol. 3, Fall 1971, pp. 161-171.

Woodward, W. R., "Scientific Genius and Loss of a Parent," *Science Studies*, July 1974, Vol. 4, pp. 265-

WORKING CONSTRUCTIVELY WITH THE DYING OR BEREAVED CHILD

Preparatory Understanding of Death
The Young Child

by
*Elizabeth F. Young**

"Mommy, what does 'dead' mean? Why did Jimmy die? Where did he go? Will I die, too?"

When confronted with these and similar questions—many parents of small children are tempted to answer evasively, to avoid further discussion of the subject. Indeed, some authorities allege that death has replaced sex as *the* taboo subject for family conversation. Many small nuclear families, removed from family support and relationships with the aged, have little experience with death and grief and feel helpless and uncertain as to what to say. The tremendous amount of anxiety about death which is such a prominent part of our death-denying culture, makes it even more difficult for parents to respond to such questions.[1] Parents project their anxiety and emotions onto the child, assuming that the question is as complicated for him, as full of emotional repercussions, as it is for themselves, when perhaps all the child wants is a simple factual answer. A very young child may only want to know that to be dead is to be unable to move, or perhaps that Jimmy died of a certain disease, or what coffins or cemeteries are for. Of course, an older child may want to discuss some of the more complicated philosophical and emotional implications of death. By the way his parent hesitates or changes his tone of voice when the subject of death is introduced into the conversation, the child learns that this subject is very different from any other. Children need direct, simple information about death, as about any thing else. In addition, they need continuing reassurance as they try to understand, because the subject of death *is* different and difficult.

Most of us are well aware of our inadequacies when faced with such questions from our children. A few are completely sure of their beliefs. Some are certain that there is an afterlife; others are equally sure that death is the end of everything. But most of us are not so sure. We are torn by doubts and questionings, yet we realize full well the finality and awesome mystery of death, know that it is life's constant companion, to be faced with courage and wonder as a fact of life—its opposite. Most of the time, we

---

*Ms. Young is a teacher of pre-schoolers in Palo Alto, California.

convey these feelings to our children quite unconsciously and unintentional-ly, but there are certain experiences, explorations and understandings that we may give them intentionally. Thus, we may prepare them to accept the inevitability of death and enable them to face the death of someone dear, whenever it may occur, with as little trauma as possible.

To force ourselves to think of death as a reality and to come to terms with it ourselves is the first and major step. Only as we learn to live with death can we help our children to do so. If I had to choose a single word to encompass all the aspects of this desired attitude toward death, that word would be "awareness": awareness of feelings, of self, of otherness, of opposites, of nature, of death itself.

Children are no strangers to feelings. They know what it means to be mad, sad, glad, guilty, afraid, lonely. They know how it feels to be separated from others and to need forgiveness. They express their feelings naturally and are very quick to sense adult feelings—of excitement over a new car, a shopping trip, a vacation, of anxiety over loss of job, prospects of moving, illness in the family; of sadness, particularly in the mother. They are sensitive to loud, angry talk or whispered conversations broken off at their approach. Therefore, experiences that profoundly affect the family should be shared or explained as simply as possible so that the child does not feel that the anger or anxiety is directed at him or that he is the cause of it. A child who doesn't know the real reason for his parent's emotional state is quick to invent one out of his limited experience. Some children have lived for years with weird misconceptions, with fear and guilt which could have been prevented with a few words of explanation.

Frequently, children speak of the fear and distress they feel at night lying in bed listening to parents quarrel. Often the child misinterprets innocent arguments. One little girl of ten told me she wanted to ride away on her bike and never come back when she heard her parents fighting. She couldn't of course, so she hid her head under the covers. Young children also speak of good feelings at night, feelings of comfort and security which come from quiet bedtime talk and loving care. Two poems by Dorothy Aldis[2] express these feelings.

Going to Sleep	I Never Hear
The safest feeling	*I never hear my mother come*
In the world	*Into my room late, late at night*
Is to be lying	*She says she has to look and see*
Warm and curled	*If I'm still tucked exactly right.*
In bed while in	*Nor do I feel her kissing me;*
The room next door	*She says she does though,*
They talk; and then	*Every night.*
Don't anymore. . . .	

Obviously, children experience all kinds of feelings, but they don't always understand them. How can we help them understand? Feelings must be accepted for what they are. There must be no family cover-up campaign, no expressions like "nice people have only nice emotions." We must explore ways of expressing feelings honestly.

One way is through physical action. Each of us has a favorite activity, such as digging in the garden or slamming pots and pans around the kitchen when we are upset. We can teach a child to pound a pillow, shout, run around the block. I knew a boy once who had a 'mad' table, an old thing his father had given him that he could pound, cut, gouge, or what ever.

Feelings can also be released through different artistic media—clay, paints, finger paints, music. When our son was young, we could always tell his mood because he would go to the piano to express his feelings through music—sometimes sad, sometimes with crashing chords and dissonances mostly in the bass clef, gradually growing more quiet and moving up the keyboard till he was apparently restored to himself again.

Another way to express feelings is to talk them out with someone who will listen and understand. It is helpful to call a feeling by its name, to say, "I'm mad, sad, hurt." Denying an emotion does not make it go away. So many times we say, particularly to boys, "That doesn't hurt, you mustn't cry," or, worse still, "Boys don't cry." Such denial not only drives the bad feeling inside where it may come out later in some unexpected or undesirable manner, but it is also dishonest. It *does* hurt; they *are* sad or mad; and why shouldn't they cry? Men and boys need to cry as much as women do.

However, the crying of adults is often very disturbing to children who witness it, usually because they have never seen an adult cry. It would be much better if they had. Major concerns of the family should be the understanding and acceptance of the feelings of each member and a growing ability to feel comfortable with uncomfortable emotions. These will be of untold value in handling sorrow and grief in later life.

Feelings can also be expressed through touch. When children are angry, they frequently hit out in some sort of physical manner, but the opposite feelings of gentleness and tenderness often go unexpressed. In an attempt to restore expression through touch, much emphasis has recently been put on sensitivity training of various kinds. But the gentle hand, the hug, the touch on the shoulder; these have always been with us.

The process of understanding feelings, our own and others, is a life-long one. We can begin to help children find a common thread. When do I feel this way? What or who makes me feel this way? Is it always the same person or situation? Why do I react the way I do? How might I express my feelings in a more constructive way? How might I change the situation or find a way to handle it? How much of this feeling is necessary, or helpful, or unavoidable? How awful it would be to have no feelings!

Children must learn that many things cannot be changed; all of us have to learn to live with the "given." Sometimes, we must swallow our feelings and learn to adjust to living with certain people and situations. Many pages could be written about the process of having and being a friend, about forgiveness and empathy, but for now, let's just acknowledge the importance of friendship.

Some of the most difficult feelings for children to handle are those that involve loss and separation. Often they first experience loneliness and a sense of desertion when someone they depend on goes away. Parents can help children to handle departures and separation constructively and creatively, and thereby give them some basis on which to cope with the later experiences of death.

Loneliness arises from such varied experiences as simple homesickness at camp or while visiting grandparents to more traumatic events, such as moving, divorces, accidents, illnesses, hospitalization (especially if it involves surgery), loss or death of a pet, or death of a friend or relative. Obviously, emotional responses to these conditions will vary from child to child. Some children are more affected than others by family problems, hurt feelings, quarrels with friends or siblings, unfairness at school, home or play, punishment or being lost. These are usually the same children who react most sensitively to death.

Some children are constantly lonely because they are or feel that they are different from their peers because of race, religion, family income, or some physical handicap. Such differences may be very obvious, such as crippling from cerebral palsy, blindness, deafness, retardation, fatness, a stutter, or they may be less obvious such as unusually high intelligence, poverty, an emotional disturbance or a neurological handicap. It is those whose handicaps are invisible who suffer most from man's inhumanity to man. Some have *literally no friends!* Anything that can depersonalize causes loneliness; when our defenses are down, we are most open to hurt—and to love.

Being alone may or may not cause loneliness. Many children with working parents left alone and on their own for untold hours, often locked out of the house, seem quite happy in their own pursuits or spend this time at friends or neighbors. The real tragedy lies in the fact that some spend it in anguished waiting and others in various kinds of mischief or delinquent behavior. A sensitive chillling evocation of the feelings of this type of child can be found in *Cinci*, a story by Luigi Pirandello.[3] Other children are alone when they are in bed (often for unnecessary hours while parents want to be alone or are too lazy to get up), when they are being punished or are in trouble, when parents are out, when riding their bikes, when reading, when at camp, when in a hospital or sick at home, while working on hobbies or watching TV. Whether these "alone" times relieve or intensify loneliness depends on the child and his particular situation.

Children's responses vary as much as the conditions. They may show great anxiety or guilt, fear of desertion, loss of love, rejection. They respond by withdrawal, with self pity, bitterness, or anger; they may become wary or defiant, delinquent, or emotionally disturbed. Many conditions beyond their control, such as father without a job, mother crying, parents quarreling, having too much responsibility too soon, or too much exposure to adult life too young, may lead to great insecurity, anxiety or apathy. Their most desperate need is for understanding, someone to talk to, someone to listen! Far from being uncommon, loneliness is the "given" with which many of our children live.

Time spend alone can be very rewarding. A generation ago, children could spend hours walking in the woods, lying on their backs in the fields or orchards, just dreaming. Children have little opportunity to wander in nature today. There is too much hustle and bustle everywhere, too many fences and too many "Private Property—Keep Out" signs. Instead, it seems to me today's children are furnished with too much artificial entertainment. As parents, we need to plan for them to have time alone in nature, to have pets, to cultivate hobbies or other creative activities. Children also need time and solitude to daydream and fantasize, to cry, to pray, to realize God's presence.

In his monograph on loneliness,[4] Clark Moustakas, who has worked with children as a therapist and teacher for many years at the Merrill Palmer School in Detroit, has this to say:

Feelings of loneliness must often be hidden in childhood. They are too frightening and disturbing—like any intense, severe, disturbing emotion these feelings must be curbed, controlled, denied, or, if expressed, quickly resolved or eliminated through busy activities and goals. Children become afraid early to let others know how they actually feel. The natural and inevitable loneliness resulting in childhood must be distorted and controlled in interactions with others. The child soon believes that he can show his parents only an expurgated, carefully edited version of his inner life. He begins to suffer deep feelings of guilt and inadequacy as he learns to regard his loneliness as "bad" and as a kind of sickness. The natural loneliness of inner life becomes confounded and confused, and sometimes the child enters into the tragic loneliness anxiety of self-alienation. For this reason it is important to give children an opportunity to express their feelings of loneliness. It is one way to break through the terrible sense of guilt and isolation.

Moustakas continues that we need to distinguish rather clearly between loneliness and loneliness anxiety. He states, what has been confirmed by many others, that loneliness is also the source of creativity and is to be highly cherished. We have to be alone to find ourselves, to think, to create, to relate to God. But very often the only times children are alone are when they are being punished or isolated for some negative reason or at just the times they do not know how to handle.

Parents can help children prepare for both pleasant and unpleasant solitude. They can talk about the problems, try to instill a sense of adventure about moving and making new friends, try to understand and accept differences in themselves and other people. All of us need to learn how to release our feelings rather than nurse them. We also need to realize that sometimes we have to just be and endure the loneliness in whatever form it comes. We need to develop inner resources, and our own individual ways of coping creatively.

This discussion of solitude leads to the next point—the child's need to become aware of himself, of his dreams, his thoughts and his feelings. This self-awareness develops best in solitude. Each one of us has to realize that he is an individual and that individuality is one of the major blessings of life. We each have different gifts, different ways of thinking, different characteristics that might be called handicaps—perhaps our height, the color of our hair, freckles, or perhaps something much deeper than such physical traits. Here again we have to learn to live with the given. Some things can not be changed.

We also need to help children grow in inner resourcefulness so that each can say, "I did it! I can do it myself!" A child may feel a sense of accomplishment from a very simple act, perhaps from finding the courage to go to bed alone at night in a dark room, to walk past a house where a dog is barking, to go to the dentist, to be innoculated without crying, to wear glasses. Or the accomplishment may demand greater inner strength such as when the child is sick or alone in the hospital and is able to summon from his own little being the courage to get through the situation.

Children can grow in moral courage. When they can confess guilt and accept the consequences, they increase their inner strength. They may admit to losing a library book, or breaking a window, or knocking over one of mother's plants—the list is endless. But if they have the courage to say, "I did it," then they have grown.

Children also grow in trustworthiness. They can be old enough to watch the baby for a few minutes or to practice a lesson when no one is home, in other words, to be able to be responsible for their own actions when parent or teacher is not there. They also grow in ability to make difficult decisions, to choose between doing something already promised and accepting a sudden invitation to an outing with friends, to decide to tell or not to tell when they see someone cheating or stealing. Experience and guidance in making difficult decisions helps the child grow in self-awareness.

Once the child begins growing towards awareness of himself, perhaps even before this, he can begin to have experiences of what I will call "otherness," an awareness of all the intangibles that are in our lives and yet beyond us. Often it seems that children are much closer to this sense of otherness than adults. As Wordsworth said so beautifully, "Still trailing clouds of glory they do come from God who is their home." Maybe this quality is what Jesus meant when he said, "Unless ye become as little children, ye shall not enter the Kingdom of Heaven." I think we all know the quality I am referring to; it is more than innocence; it is a sense of still being in touch with God. Throughout history this quality of otherness has been found in seers, prophets, shamans, priestesses, mediums, sibyls, witches, artists, poets, musicians. It is the ability to mediate between the conscious and unconscious, to express an awareness of all that the universe is.

One aspect of otherness with which children are most familiar is shadows. Children seem to have as great an interest and delight in their shadows as that described in writings about primitive people. Laurens Van der Post, in many of his writings, speaks of the Bushmen's age-old feelings about shadows: how important they are to their sense of well-being, how their image of dying is that of losing their shadows. He writes in *The Heart of the Hunter*[5] about Dabe, an old Bushman, who had a severe asthma attack one night. When Van der Post went to see him the next morning, Dabe was gone from his bed. Hearing a strange noise outside, he looked out the window:

> It was Dabe, standing sideways, fully dressed, his hat in his hand and his head turned over his shoulder, eyes fixed on his own shadow which in that light lay like ink on the crimson sand and stretched to just beyond the far end of the compound. The voice which made the noise was not at all Dabe's normal one but hoarse, oddly authoritative and deep, as if it came with the beat of an incantation from the pit of his stomach.
> "Who is he," the voice chanted, "who stands here in the morning sun?"
> "Who is he with so tall a shadow beside him?"

"Whose shadow is this that starts at sunrise and ends at sunset?"
"Who is he who has an ostrich feather in his hat?"
"Who is he who puts the hat on the bare head of the shadow?"
The voice paused while Dabe clamped firmly on his head the ridiculous European hat he insisted on wearing. Then he resumed, deeper than ever on a big drum-like note:
"Why Dabe, you child of Bushman you! It is you!" And with that he danced a sprightly step or two.

Children share the primitive man's fascination with shadows. To be able to make one's shadow larger or smaller at will, yet not be able to lose it, is a visible, available and partially controllable experience of otherness. To step on each other's shadows, to climb shadow trees and walk along shadow roof tops, on the ground, is wonderful fun. We have all indulged in various forms of shadow play—with our hands, with puppets, with tableaus, with silhouettes. Without realizing it, we depend on shadows to tell us the time of day and the seasons of the year, and to judge position of objects, movement and depth.

Children also experience otherness through their dreams, Parents need to help them be aware of their dreams and to talk about them without trying to interpret them. Children do have good dreams, but parents usually hear only about their nightmares. Daydreaming and fantasizing are experiences of otherness we all indulge in.

Thoughts and memories are true otherness, completely intangible but indispensable. Sara Teasdale[6] has written a charming poem about memories:

The Coin

Into my heart's treasury
I slipped a coin
That time cannot take
Nor a thief purloin —
Oh, better than the minting
Of a gold-crowned king
Is the safe-kept memory
Of a lovely thing.

Children also seem to excel in another indispensable facet of otherness—imagination. Their imaginings take many different forms. Children create tall tales of imaginary playmates; fact and fancy lie very close together in young children. They delight us with fresh, uninhibited views of the world and the people in it, whether expressed in conversation or through other media, such as drawing, finger painting, collages, clay, music, dance.

Solitude is an essential part of otherness, providing time for the awareness of the complete otherness of God—the soul, the spirit, all the intangibles that are involved in who and what we are.

Probably one of the best ways to promote a sense of wonder and mystery in children's lives is to explore nature, experience its diversity and beauty, its dependability and unpredictability, its vastness and closeness in all its myriad forms. Even the commonest things, such as salt, seeds, our hands, reflect this wonder. Children respond, again, in much the same way as primitives to the great forces of nature; they seem to sense its wholeness in a way we have lost.

One of the most fascinating phenomena of nature is light, which gives shape and beauty to all we see, with its ever changing colors and shadows. The sources of light—the sun, moon, and stars—are all influential in children's lives. Piaget has found that it is the sun and moon to which children attribute life and motion long after they have discarded them in relation to other things. Study the stars with your children. Experiment with color and the effects of light.

Then there is the wind (Oh, the joy of flying a kite!), invisible, uncontrollable, again with many primitive connotations of life and death, with the tremendous power of storm, cyclone, tornado, etc.; thunder and lightning; fire; water in all its myriad forms—rain, snow, ice, hail, lakes, streams, oceans, waterfalls, glaciers, geysers. When we are dealing with some of these implacable forces of nature, we must remember that they can be very disturbing and frightening to children, partly because they are so vast and powerful, partly because they are so impersonal. We should try to balance them with the miniatures in nature, such as bugs, snails, snowflakes, diatoms, butterflies, each of which has infinite variety of form, shape, and color. Children are greatly comforted by learning that at the time of dinosaurs, butterflies existed, too. This need to balance the immensity of the universe with the intimacy of small things is expressed for us again by Sara Teasdale.[7]

Full Moon
(Santa Barbara)

I listened, there was not a sound to hear
  In the great rain of moonlight pouring down,
The eucalyptus trees were carved in silver,
  And a light mist of silver lulled the town.

I saw far off the great Pacific bearing
  A broad white disk of flame,
And on the garden-walk a snail beside me
  Tracing in crystal the slow way he came.

Another area to explore is sound. Become aware of sounds, both natural and man-made. Is there ever true silence except in a laboratory situation or for the totally deaf? Listen to the insects, birds, wind, movements of creatures, as well as all the machine noises of our environment. Imagine what one might hear in the Arctic or the desert. Van der Post and others speak frequently of the sound of the stars in the vast silence of the desert. Imagine how man developed his awareness of noise and music; how he started with no other instruments than his own voice and body (still today in parts of Africa and Australia we find what is called "body percussion"—the many sounds that can be made by slapping different parts of the body); how he used whatever was in his particular environment to make drums, rattles, whistles and other woodwinds, and finally, strings. Explore body percussion with your children and try making different kinds of instruments.

In addition to the rhythms of sound and music, there are the cyclic rhythms of nature—night and day, the seasons, the phases of the moon, the tides, the lives of seeds, insects, plants, animals, people. The dependency of life forms on each other—food chains, death in nature—are often difficult for children to understand and accept. We eat plants and animals; all creatures eat other living things. Death is a natural part of life; all things have a life span and expectancy—the cells of our bodies, plants, insects, animals, trees, radium, etc. Give children opportunities to notice and talk about dead flowers, flies, bugs, birds. Help them to participate in the cycles and ongoingness of life and learn to care for all life in its infinite variety.

Other explorations, so obvious that it almost seems foolish to mention them, are an important part of these preparatory experiences. I am referring to opposites. They may be as simple as those of place—up-down, in-out, over-under; they can be kinaesthetic—cold-hot, wet-dry, soft-hard, soft-loud, heavy-light, rough-smooth; they may be concepts—old-young, rich-poor, healthy-sick, light-dark, black-white (colors and people), sad-happy, good-evil, animated-inanimate. Here, we can help children to distinguish between stuffed animals or dolls and real pets or live babies; between manmade objects and living things. Children attribute life to anything that moves much longer than we realize and often believe, for instance, that if planted and watered, buttons and marbles will grow as seeds do. These experiences of opposites all lead up to the concept of life and death as opposites—yet one.

So let us be as sensitive as possible to feelings and situations associated with loss, separation and grief; as honest as we can when children ask questions about death. Don't be didactic, leave the door open, share the mystery and wonder; not all problems have answers. Death is a mystery we share with all mankind; death is a part of life, its opposite. Life and death go together; "in the midst of life we are in death."

The books listed below represent a sample of literature on death. Some of them provide background information for adults to clarify their thinking and feeling. Of these, Rabbi Grollman's book, "Explaining Death to Children" is a "must." Most of the books, however, are intended to be used with or by children. Some are quite specific; in others references to death are more oblique and in still others the theme of death is not at all an important part of the story, yet is handled so beautifully that it is good for children to be exposed to such interpretations. Let me suggest that, as parents, you read the books specifically about death before you use them with your child to be sure there is nothing in them that might conflict with your religious beliefs. Among the books which contain only indirect references to death, the fantasy ones appeal to me most because of their sense of mystery and wonder, their very non-reality and non-didacticism.

BOOKS FOR ADULTS ABOUT DEATH

Choron, Jacques. *Death and Western Thought*, MacMillan, 1963.
What philosophers of the Western World, from Socrates to Sartre, have thought about death. Difficult reading, but interesting.

Feifel, Herman. *The Meaning of Death*, Mc-Graw-Hill, 1959.
One of the first books to offer insights into the meaning of death from the viewpoint of different disciplines. Very helpful.

Mills, Liston. *Perspectives on Death*. Abingdon, 1969.
Death as seen in the Old and New Testaments with subsequent interpretation by the church; death in contemporary literature; as a psychological and social event; the ethical and pastoral problems with the dying and bereaved.

Green, Judith S. *Laughing Souls: The Days of the Dead in Oaxaca, Mexico*. San Diego Museum, 1969.
Warm, family celebration in a different culture.

Grollman, Earl. *Explaining Death to Children*, Beacon Press, 1967.
An absolute "must" for parents, ministers, and all who work with children. Another invaluable multidisciplinary approach. Three fine chapters on the concerns and attitudes of the Roman Catholic, Protestant, and Jewish traditions.

Kübler-Ross, Elizabeth. *On Death and Dying*, MacMillan, 1969.
The first book to talk about death from the viewpoint of the dying, outlining their needs and feelings in the various stages of dying and telling how others can help them die with meaning. Written in non-technical language by a beautiful spirit.

Schoenberg, Bernard, M.D. et al. *Loss and Grief: Psychological Management in Medical Practice*, Columbia University Press, 1970.
Written for professionals but not too technical for laymen; a section on the dying child; one on partial loss such as blindness or amputation; one on handling grief.

Neale, Robert. *The Art of Dying*, Harper and Row, 1973.
A series of mental confrontations with our own death, allowing us to understand it as a natural part of life and giving that life a new dimension. A unique approach.

Moon and Howes. *And a Time to Die—Mark Pelgrin*, Contact Editions 1962.
One man's search for meaning in life as he faces his own death from cancer. A Jungian approach.

DIRECT DISCUSSION OF DEATH FOR CHILDREN

Coburn, John. *Anne and the Sand Dobbies*, Seabury Press, 1964.
An Episcopal priest discusses death of baby sister honestly and in laymen's terms. Some of this story is overly dramatic. "Sand-dobby" concept, to me, just confounds and complicates the mystery, raising more questions than it answers. Read first.

Harris, Audrey. *Why Did He Die?* Lerner Publications Co., 1965.
Recommended by Dr. Ross. Emphasis on kind of life, memories live on, people wear out, we are sad but must move on. Some of the answers are overly sure.

Miles, Miska. *Annie and the Old One*, Little, Brown & Co., 1971.
A beautiful story of a little Indian girl who tries to postpone her grandmother's death. Simply told with the emphasis on love and wonder; death is all right, life goes on.

Viorst, Judith. *The Tenth Good Thing About Barney*, Atheneum, 1971.
Honest, sensitive response to the death of a pet. Time heals, life goes on, things change; end might be frightening or distasteful to some sensitive children.

Warburg, Sandol. *Growing Time*, Houghton Mifflin, 1969.
Understanding, responsive adults help a boy to face reality of his dog's death and to accept the continuity of life. Perhaps the new puppy is brought too soon; otherwise good.

BOOKS CONTAINING INDIRECT REFERENCES TO DEATH

Alcott Louisa May. *Little Men, Little Women*, in a variety of editions.
The deaths of family members are treated with love and tenderness.

Blegvad, Lenore. *Moon-watch Summer*, Harcourt, Brace, Jovanovich, 1972.
About a boy who discovers that seeing how people and things around him live, grow, feel and die is more important than watching the moon walks.

Musgrave, Florence. *Marged*, Farrar, Straus & Co., 1956.
A young girl who loses her parents in a flood, bitterly blames her grandmother, then finally realizes that they are together in their suffering.

Saint-Exupery, Antoine de. *The Little Prince*, Harcourt Brace, 1943.
A "must" book for you and your children when they are ready. To be read and reread with different insights each time. About loneliness,

aloneness, gentleness, mystery, wonder, life and death. "What is essential is invisible to the eye (it is only with the heart that one sees rightly)."

Cunningham, Julia. *Burnish Me Bright*, Pantheon Books, 1970.
A strange story of a deafmute who learns to mime, of loneliness and love, of life and death. Almost as mystical as "The Little Prince."

L'Engle, Madeleine. *A Wrinkle in Time*, Farrar, Straus & Co., 1962.
A science fiction story appealing to modern children; about good vs. evil, life vs. death, the triumph of love over IT.

MacDonald, George. *At the Back of the North Wind*, The MacMillan Co., 1964.
A mystical story of a small boy's adventures with the north wind which culminates in his death.

Zimnik, Reiner. *The Bear and the People*, Harper & Row Publications, 1950.
A gentle dreamlike story about a dancing bear, a silver horn and a tiny melody that echoes through the years. About life and death, love and people.

BOOKS ABOUT FEELINGS

Fahs and Hills. *Martin and Judy*, 3 vols., Beacon Press, 1950.
Experiences for preschoolers with shadows, dreams, snow, wind, babies.

Wensborg and Northrup. *The Tuckers*, Beacon Press, 1952.
Similar stories for 1-3 graders. Adult guide. Excellent material on invisibility and death.

Fahs and Spoerl. *Beginnings* (of Life, Death, Earth and Sky). Beacon Press, 1950.
Carefully selected myths from many cultures. Marvelous discussion of children's wonderings about life and death. Especially good for a group. These stories, either written or planned by Sophia Fahs, show an understanding of children and an ability to create feelings of wonder about life and death. They put words to thoughts and feelings that children are unable to express and truly exemplify the awareness of which I have been speaking. Using these stories with children first started me toward a realization of the importance of these awarenesses.

These four books express the beauty and wonders of God and his world three of them with photographs, the other with Weisgard's inimitable illustrations having the softness of brush paintings.

Atwood, Ann. *New Moon Cove*, Chas. Scribner's Sons, 1967.
　Effects of light on color, shapes, shadows, Beautiful.

Carson, Rachel. *The Sense of Wonder*, Harper & Row Publishers, 1965.
　Use it over and over to explore the wonders of nature. Full of wisdom
　and beauty.

Fitch, Florence. *A Book About God*, Lothrop, Lee & Shepard Co., 1953.
　A serene, beautiful book that children will love.

Gudnason, Kay. *Psalms of the Heavens, Earth and Sky*, W. A. Wilde Co.,
　1964.
　Black and white photographs illustrating excerpts from the Psalms.
　Fantastic cloud pictures.

Axline, Virginia. *Dibs—In Search of Self*, Ballentine Books, 1964.
　For parents. With loving help a child finds himself.

Berger, Terry. *I Have Feelings*, Behavioral Publications, 1971.
　For children four to nine. Good and bad feelings.

Burch and Strong. *Once There Was a Tree*. World Publishing Co., 1968.
　Cycles of life and death.

De Regniers, Beatrice. *A Little House of Your Own*, Harcourt Brace & Co.,
　1954.
　About "needing" a house of our own. To read aloud. Charming drawings.

De Regniers, Beatrice. *Shadows*, Harcourt Brace & Co., 1960.
　Fun with shadows.

Jones, Elizabeth O. *Songs of the Sun*, The MacMillan Co., 1952.
　Story of St. Francis and his song with charming pictures.

Mendoza, George. *The World from My Window*, Hawthorn Books Inc.,
　1969.
　Poems by ghetto children, some joyful, most of loneliness and despair.

Norman, Gertrude. *The First Book of Music*, F. Watts Publishing Co., 1954.
　Introduction to music and musical instruments.

O'Neill, Mary. *Hailstones and Halibut Bones*, Doubleday & Co., 1961.
　Delightful fun with colors.

Politi, Leo. *The Butterflies Come, Song of the Swallows*, Chas. Scribner's
　Sons, 1948.
　Wonders of migration.

Seredy, Kate. *A Tree for Peter*. Viking Press, 1959.
　How a gift of love from a derelict tramp brings new life and love to a
　small boy and the other dwellers on the city dump.

Silverstein, Shel. *The Giving Tree*, Harper & Row, 1964.
  About loving and giving.

Stevens, Bertha. *How Miracles Abound*, Beacon Press, 1941.
  Intelligent wondering, exploring and imagining in the world of nature.

Van Meter, Harriet. *Hands, Hands, Hands!*, John Knox Press, 1966.
  The wonder in our hands.

Warburg, Sandol. *Keep It Like a Secret*, Little, Brown & Co., 1961.
  A gift of love for a new born baby. Bright, colorful, different.

FOOTNOTES

1. See Grollman, Earl. "Explaining Death to Children," Beacon Press 1967. Article by Edgar N. Jackson, pp. 171-181.
2. From *All Together* by Dorothy Aldis, G. P. Putnam, 1939.
3. "Cinci" by Luigi Pirandello in *The Existential Imagination*, edited by Frederick R. Karl and Leo Hamalian, Fawcett Publications, 1963.
4. *Loneliness* by Clark Moustakas, Prentice-Hall, 1961.
5. Van der Post, Laurens, *The Heart of the Hunter*, Morrow, 1961.
6. *The Collected Poems of Sara Teasdale*, MacMillan Co., 1955.
7. *Ibid.*

Some Observations by a Clergyman

By Rabbi Earl Grollman

I think that very often when we deal with children, as well as adults, we, as clergymen, say the wrong things. We feel that we have to say something profound or that we must talk in the language of the Bible, rather than talking in terms of the life of the deceased and the needs of the survivors. When the clergyman walks in, and perhaps he's speaking to the boy whose father had died, he might say, "Your father died because he was a good man, and God takes those who are good." (Have you ever heard this before?)

Remember the movie, *Yours, Mine and Ours*, with Lucille Ball? In the opening scene, Lucille Ball is portrayed as a widow. Her husband has just died, and her little boy is acting up all over the place. And Lucille Ball says, "Why are you so naughty?" And the lad retorts, "Because you said God takes those who are good, and I don't want God to take me." I think the next question is, "If God takes those who are good, what are you 'mamma', doing here?" Sometimes we say, "Your father is now up in heaven." Now I'm not against the word *heaven*. But I think that we must explain this word to the youngster and be prepared for those interrogations. If "father is up in heaven," then why are you burying him in the earth? And we know of cases of children in airplanes who

This article was excerpted from a chapter by Rabbi Earl Grollman, Temple Beth-El, Belmont, Mass., which appears in HELPING EACH OTHER IN WIDOWHOOD, edited by Dr. Phyllis R. Silverman, Copyright © 1974, by Health Sciences Publishing Corp.

look up in the clouds (in heaven) seeking their deceased loved one.

Very often in our desire to give easy explanations, we bring confusion and consternation. I've heard clergymen say, "Your father is away on a long journey." The child might think; If he's "away on a long journey," why is everybody crying? The greatest fear that every child has is the fear of being abandoned. All of you who have small children might recall that when you would leave them even briefly they would cry. For them, it seemed like abandonment, death.

Or very often we say, "Your father is now asleep." Now I've read *Homer,* and I've read the *Iliad,* and *Thanatos,* and *Hypnos;* sleep and death are twin buds of the same flower. But I have known children who are afraid to go to sleep at night because they can't distinguish between real sleep and eternal sleep. I think that funeral directors, make a mistake when they call some of the rooms "slumber rooms." The person is not asleep; the person is *dead,* never to return on this earth.

I find that when I speak to young people and to older people that it is inordinately important that I not explain to them what I believe, but instead try to understand what they think. For example, I recall a television appearance which I was to make. In preparation, I asked some of the younger students of my religious school to quiz me. I said, "Death is permanent." And a little girl said, "So what?" I said, "Permanent!"

She said, "My mother has permanents; how long does a permanent last?"

Dealing with death is the most important aspect of my entire ministry. It's the one time I am really a minister;

it's one of the times that I am really needed. The telephone rings, I answer and somebody says, "Rabbi Grollman," and then there is a sob, and I know what's going to come next. No matter what is occurring, I usually say, "Where are you?" And when I do seem them, I find that the best approach is non-verbal. It is not one of verbosity, but rather of touch. I walk in and embrace the survivor. And guess what I'll say? Nothing.

I think so often we have the compulsion, especially we who are clergymen, to bring in some kind of magical formula. "It's God's will." I've heard so much garbage uttered in a house of bereavement. People believe that they have to say something abstruse. "It's God's will," and you look around, and who's the person who's saying it? It's an atheist. How do you know? She says, "Honest to God, I'm an atheist."

I will take the person's hand, sit down, and listen. Usually I hear something like this: "Here I was, and he said, 'I'm not feeling well,' and I rushed over to him, and he fell down and I went to pick him up, and I got him a glass of water, and I called the ambulance, and . . ." She goes over and over and over it again. I listen, and then somebody else walks in the room and she tells the same story again and again and again. What is she really doing? She is trying to say, "I don't believe it's really so." Or, "I really did everything that was possible." She is trying to exonerate herself in terms of guilt and recrimination.

As a clergyman I have other responsibilities. When a death occurs, very often their mother will say to me, "Will you tell the children?" My answer is "no." Is that callous? I say, "I will be with you, but we must all be together as a family unit."

Also if it is the father who has died, I advise the mother not to tell his young son that he is now the man of the family. He is *not* the man of the family. I have seen too many cases where the boy actually wants to take over the role of the father, even to the extent: "Can I now sleep with you?"

I tell the children that it is permissible, if they desire, to cry. Tears are a tribute of yearning for a person who has died. I am unhappy with the sterile approach at funerals by some clergymen who say, "Don't cry, you've got to be strong." That's nonsense. Somebody has died, and when a person dies, part of you has died with this individual. I tell the family, "If you want to cry, cry." Sometimes the youngsters are seemingly unmoved at the death. The children might say, "Oh. Can I go out now and play?" I try to explain to the survivors that it does not mean that the child did not love the departed loved one. It is so sudden that he just cannot accept the reality of death. When a child says, "Can I go out and play?" this is his way of fending it off; this is part of his mechanism of defense, of denial.

Very often the parents will say, "I don't think I should take the child to the funeral, do you? I mean, after all, I don't want to expose him." My answer is, "Why don't we find out what the child thinks?" In my book, *Explaining Death to Children,* at the age of 7, I felt a child should be able to attend a funeral. However, I now realize that no one can arbitrarily set a chronological age level. You cannot state that at a certain age a person can be present at a funeral. Certain criteria should be present. First, I think the children should know what a funeral is all about. It is unconscionable to take a child to a funeral if he does not know what is going to happen. This is one reason why I wrote a book called *Talking About Death for Children* (Grollman, 1970). When my children went to the hospital to have a tonsillectomy, we would take out a little book called *When Johnny Goes to the Hospital.* But when they go to a funeral, it is shrouded in mysticism. Clergymen have a responsibility to speak to the children and explain what a funeral is.

We have a funeral director come into our temple and explain to the youth what they might expect in terms of caskets, funeral homes, and embalming. As a clergyman, I sit down with the family and explain the procedure.

Secondly, I try to elicit from the young person himself whether he wants to attend, not making him feel guilty if he prefers not to attend. The decision is his. Very often the parent will say, "You don't have to," which means, "don't go."

As a clergyman, I speak in terms of forgiveness. God forgives you, but will you forgive yourself? I think the whole idea of forgiveness and our religious resources can help to soften some of these people who are so burdened by this tremendous amount of guilt and recrimination. And I find, especially with children, the guilt is tremendously great, because children believe in crime and punishment. If a child does something good, we say, "Ah, you're a good boy, you can watch television tonight." Or, "You've been bad. You don't go to the movies on Sunday." So I discover that when death happens the child begins to think in his own mind, "What did I do wrong?" A child thinks in terms of the omnipotence of words. "One time . . . I said, 'drop dead'." He thinks because he said "drop dead," that this is why it happened. I try to work with the child, and also with the parent, (because parents are really children, only they're more sophisticated). Wishing doesn't make it so; the person died for lots of reasons.

I try to allow the person to walk through "the valley of the shadow." As a clergyman I believe (and I represent the liberal wing), in customs and ceremonials dealing with death. To carry out traditions and ceremonials related to death is also saying, "I didn't do everything I could in life, but I sure can do it now." In my congregation, there are people who come to the Temple every single morning at 7:00 to say the mourner's prayers as is prescribed in Jewish Law for the entire mourning period (11 months). As I counsel them and work with them, I find that many of these people really feel guilty. By going to the Temple they're doing something at the time of death which they did not always do during their loved one's life. In addition, they hear from others: "Isn't he a wonderful son," because of the fact that they come each morning. Customs, ceremonials, and traditions do help us in times of adversity. It was Margaret Mead, who said, "When a person is born we rejoice, and when they're married we jubilate, but when they die, we try to pretend that nothing has happened." Customs and ceremonials give us some kind of drama, as well as a link with history.

Helping Children Cope With Death*

By Edgar N. Jackson, D.D.

Death is a part of natural order. The casual observer can see it all around in plant and animal life. But underlying death there is another order, the phenomenon of ever-renewed life. For the individual, death in general does not usually present the problem that a specific death produces. To a parent, one of the more difficult educational tasks is that of helping a child to develop the insight and the resources to cope with the specific death that becomes a part of his experience.

To help a child take a healthful approach to the fact of death, the first thing that an adult must do is to come to terms with his own fears and feelings on the subject. The barrier to communication is usually more emotional than verbal. When he has sorted out his own feelings, he feels freer to talk without restraint to the child who comes to him laden with questions.

When should you talk to a child about death? Usually a child will show his interest in the subject directly. It may appear in playing hospital, in playing war, or in playing with toy guns. His games are explorative behavior to see how he feels about ideas. Or he may make comments and ask questions that show he is thinking about the subject. Some event in the family, in the neighborhood, or in the news may precipitate the question. It may be filled with emotion or merely with curiosity. But most often the child raises the question of death when his interest or experience is confronted by it.

What kinds of questions do children ask? Usually they are closely related to experience. They may include imagination or show the emotional climate that surrounds the experience. But usually they are simple and direct efforts to satisfy curiosity and gain information. The question should be answered in the mood in which it is asked. If the child seeks simple information and is greeted with an avalanche of emotion, he will have difficulty relating the answer to the question. For him it may seem unanswered, and the anxiety related to the asking of it will remain.

That is the time for answers. Evasion creates apprehension. This starts the process of adding an unwarranted emotional dimension to

---

* Dr. Jackson is the former pastor of Mamaroneck Methodist Church, New York, and the Chairman, Advisory Board, Guidance Center of New Rochelle, N.Y.

the simple question, and may make it difficult or impossible to ask more. The simple and direct answer dispels anxiety and gives confidence that the subject is not taboo and can be explored.

One of the hazards most adults encounter in these situations is their own tendency to overanswer. They complicate the problem by trying to answer their own questions rather than by adhering only to the question the child asks. It is better to ask the child questions that can sharpen and clarify his interest rather than to overanswer. Just asking "How do you mean?" or, if the question is quite general, "Just what was it you wanted to know?" may be all that is needed to clarify matters. Often the adult's apprehension about death adds much more to the question than the child had in mind. Overanswering may well be the indication of anxiety, and the child is far more responsive to the anxiety than he is to the complicated answer.

What should you tell a child about death? The answer to this question is related to the age of the child, the nature of the event, and the degree of his interest in it. He may be flooded inside with questions. These indicate the growing depth of his thought and feeling. He should be made to feel comfortable in his asking. He should be made to feel that the fact of death can be dealt with competently by people around him. While he may well be aware of the emotional content of the experience—for those around him may not be able to hide their feelings—he also should feel that they are not helpless facing the event.

Honest answers are important to a child. Children have a built-in lie detector; a child senses it when he is not getting a truthful answer. This tends to compound his anxiety, for then, not only is he not getting the answers he needs, but also he is finding some emotions he does not need. He feels insecure with adults who are afraid of his questions. He feels threatened by the feeling that his communication with others has broken down. He may not know how to explain it, but when he has more questions, he may not want to ask them of an unsatisfactory source, and thereupon he withdraws into his own thoughts or looks elsewhere for answers.

Young children have no sense of time or distance. The house on the corner seems a long way off. The now is important, and a day or a week or a month are indistinguishable. The approach to life is largely emotional. When an important person is gone from that life, it is important to fill in the blank spot with emotional warmth and added security until the child adapts to the differences. For an older child, curiosity may be added to the feeling of deprivation, and he may ask questions that show he is trying to understand what death is like physically. He wants to clarify his understanding of how death is different from life. Or he may ask questions that show he wants to know what difference death makes in the variety of human relations.

The teenager, filled with a new sense of the creative power of life and the wonder of the future, shows his interest in the subect by a quest for the spiritual, psychological, and personal meanings of death. He is busily engaged in welding his philosophy of life and needs to have a place into which death will fit. The teenager who is most apt to need special help is the one who cannot talk about death when it occurs. He is probably indicating that he cannot cope with the idea, and his *philosophy of life is not big enough* to find a place for it.

Children and young people are a help to the adults around them in encouraging an open and honest discussion of events. Their questions are apt to be direct and forthright. This makes it easier for the adult to come to terms with his own thoughts and feelings at the same time that he is trying to understand and answer properly the queries of the child.

Often questions are raised as to the participation of children in funerals and the other ceremonial events that surround death. We need to recognize that the funeral is not merely the religious service, but is also all of the events from the time of death through the interment, in which the religious and social community participates. It involves the planning, the visitations, the coming together of the family and the emotional support of the neighbors. Naturally, the child knows that something unusual is going on and he wants to be a part of it. While he may not know the fuller meaning of the events, he does want to participate to the extent that he can understand them. While it would never be wise to force a child to do things he finds threatening or unacceptable, he should be made comfortable in participating in the event up to the limits of his ability. He can understand his inclusion far better than he can understand his exclusion. If he is old enough to go to church, he is old enough to go to a funeral. If he is curious about what goes on at the funeral home, it would be better to satisfy his curiosity rather than to surround it with an emptiness that his imagination would fill. In addition, it might be helpful to take the child to the funeral home when there are few people around and no service is in progress, so that his questions can be answered freely. In this way, he meets the event openly and honestly. The anxiety is reduced at the same time that his understanding increases.

Basically, a child should be helped to see that natural death is not tragic. Although it brings changes to life, that life is supported by a faith that man's spirit is not obliterated by anything incidental to his physical nature. However, he should be taught from the circumstances surrounding unnatural and untimely death that man has responsibilities toward himself and others. In order to live the full and abundant life, he must avoid behavior that is careless, sinful, and ignorant both in himself and in others.

When this is done, death is not separated from life and man's responsibility. He does not then blame God for what is the unwise action of men. Rather, death becomes a significant event in the personal history of all mortal creatures that must ultimately be faced. The way of life that lives always as if it were aware of this fact tends to be more spiritually mature and morally conscious. So, in truth, we can learn much about the facts of life from the facts of death. Then, and perhaps only then, does our religious faith become fully relevant, for it is a faith that does not shun death, but makes even of this event a time for witness and an evidence of faith in those qualities of being that survive physical dissolution.